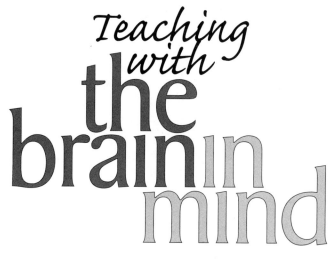

Teaching with the brain in mind

Eric Jensen

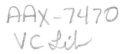

ASCD

Association for Supervision and Curriculum Development
Alexandria, Virginia USA

ASCD™

Association for Supervision and Curriculum Development
1703 N. Beauregard St. • Alexandria, VA 22311-1714 USA
Telephone: 1-800-933-2723 or 703-578-9600 • Fax: 703-575-5400
Web site: http://www.ascd.org • E-mail: member@ascd.org

Gene R. Carter, *Executive Director*
Michelle Terry, *Assistant Executive Director, Program Development*
Nancy Modrak, *Director, Publishing*
John O'Neil, *Acquisitions Editor*
Mark Goldberg, *Development Editor*
Julie Houtz, *Managing Editor of Books*
Jo Ann Irick Jones, *Senior Associate Editor*
René Bahrenfuss, *Copy Editor*
Stephanie Justen, *Proofreader*
Charles D. Halverson, *Project Assistant*
Gary Bloom, *Director, Editorial, Design, and Production Services*
Karen Monaco, *Senior Designer*
Tracey A. Smith, *Production Manager*
Dina Murray, *Production Coordinator*
John Franklin, *Production Coordinator*
Barton, Matheson, Willse & Worthington, *Desktop Publisher*

ASCD publications present a variety of viewpoints. The views expressed or implied
in this book should not be interpreted as official positions of the Association.

Printed in the United States of America.

April 1998 member book (pcr). ASCD Premium, Comprehensive, and Regular
members periodically receive ASCD books as part of their membership benefits.
No. FY98-6.

ASCD Stock No.: 198019
ASCD member price: $17.95   nonmember price: $21.95

Library of Congress Cataloging-in-Publication Data

Jensen, Eric.
        Teaching with the brain in mind / Eric Jensen.
            p.   cm.
        Includes bibliographical references and index.
        ISBN 0-87120-299-9 (pbk.)
            1. Learning, Psychology of.   2. Teaching—Psychological aspects.
        3. Brain.   I. Title.
        LB1060.J46   1998
        370.15'23—dc21   97-45424
                                                                               CIP

02 01 00 99   8 7 6 5 4 3

Dedication

To my colleagues in the brain-compatible movement: Renate and Geoffrey Caine, Jane Healy, Leslie Hart, Susan Kovalik, David Sousa, Robert Sylwester, and Pat Wolfe. Also thank-you's to William Greenough, Dolly Lambdin, Larry Squire, Pamela Moses, Katherine Roe, and Norman Weinberger for their technical review. Much gratitude to Ron Brandt for his commitment to this topic. Appreciation to Karen Markowitz for her research and editorial contributions and to Mark Goldberg for his support and editing. And many thanks to my wife Diane for her priceless support.

Teaching with
the Brain in Mind

Introduction

I first discovered the concept of "brain-compatible learning" during a business development workshop facilitated by Marshall Thurber, a futurist and entrepreneur, in June 1980. The impact was so powerful that even today, almost two decades later, I can fill the page of a flip chart with ideas I remember (and still use!). Without a doubt, both the content and process of that day were deeply embedded in my brain. The presenters clearly understood—and knew how to use—important principles about learning and the brain.

After that day, I became so enthusiastic (some would say a zealot) that I decided to share my excitement with others. Because I was teaching, my first response was, "Why don't my own students have this kind of learning experience every day?" The question was both humbling and promising.

I decided to use this newfound brain/learning connection. I cofounded an experimental, cutting-edge academic program in San Diego, California, called SuperCamp. Our purpose was to use the latest research on the brain to empower teens with life skills and learning tools. We held our first session in August 1982. It was an immediate success, and we offered it in other states and countries. We were flooded with media attention and soon found ourselves in *USA Today* and *The Wall Street Journal.* Later, we appeared on CNN and "Good Morning America."

Long-term follow-up research validated that the benefits of our program lasted years after the 10-day program itself (DePorter and Hernacki 1992, p. 19). Students' grades and school participation went up, and the students reported greater self-confidence. The experiment we began years ago is now an international fixture with more than 20,000 graduates. Today it's still growing and based in Oceanside, California.

I have seen, felt, and heard firsthand the difference brain-compatible learning makes. Students of all backgrounds and ages, with every imaginable history of failure, and with lifelong discouraged attitudes can and have succeeded with this approach. While brain-compatible learning is not a panacea, it does provide some important guidance as we move into the 21st century. Programs that are compatible with the way humans naturally learn will stand the test of time. The principles of brain-compatible learning will flourish when many other fad-like educational programs have long faded from memory.

1 The New Winds of Change

KEY CONCEPTS

▶ **Background and theory update on brain research**

▶ **The state and direction of research today**

▶ **Tools for learning about the brain**

▶ **How to interpret the new brain research**

We are on the verge of a revolution: the application of important new brain research to teaching and learning. This revolution will change school start times, discipline policies, assessment methods, teaching strategies, budget priorities, classroom environments, use of technology, and even the way we think of the arts and physical education. But before we consider the practical applications of this research, we must have a useful model for deciphering it.

Models of Education

The educational model that dominated much of human history was uncomplicated. If you wanted to learn about something, you became an apprentice to someone who possessed skills or knowledge in that area. The path was simple: find people who knew more than you and learn from them. This worked for peasants and royalty, parents and children, blacksmiths and monks.

The Industrial Revolution changed this path. A new model soon emerged with the notion that you could bring everyone together in a single place and offer a standardized, "conveyor belt" curriculum.

This paradigm of schooling was developed in the 1800s and popularized throughout most of the 20th century. Often called the "factory model," it drew from fields of sociology, business, and religion. It emphasized useful skills like obedience, orderliness, unity, and respect for authority.

A peculiar twist to this paradigm emerged during the 1950s and 1960s. In those decades, the dominant theory of human behavior was influenced by the doctrines of psychologists John Watson and B.F. Skinner. Their behaviorist theories went something like this: "We may not know what goes on inside the brain, but we can certainly see what happens on the outside. Let's measure behaviors and learn to modify them with behavior reinforcers. If we like it, reward it. If we don't, punish it." Considering what we knew about the brain at that time, this approach made some sense.

Recently, a new paradigm began emerging. History will likely record that it began in the final two decades of the 20th century. Technology paved the way for this paradigm shift; it changed the way we think, live, and learn. In the 1970s, 1980s, and 1990s, phrases like "super learning" and "accelerated learning" became mainstream as the Information Age blossomed. "Brain scanners" like Magnetic Resonance Imaging (MRI) and Positron Emission Tomography (PET) gave us new ways to understand and see inside the brain. For the first time in history, we could analyze the brain while its owner was still alive. A new breed of "inner science" developed: neuroscience, which is an exciting interdisciplinary approach to questions about the brain.

In 1969, 500 neuroscientists were registered in the International Society of Neuroscience. Today, more than 30,000 are members. A bonanza of neuroscience discoveries now reveals astonishing insights about the brain and learning. Schizophrenia and Tourette's syndrome can be treated with medication. We are closing in on the causes of Parkinson's and Alzheimer's diseases. The ability to walk again after a spinal cord injury is becoming a very real possibility. A memory pill, Nimodipine, helps students better recall what they read. We now know the biological roots of impulsive and violent classroom behavior. Many of our conventional educational beliefs are being shattered like glass.

How Do We Learn About the Brain?

We are learning about the brain at an unprecedented rate. Jeri Janowsky, a top learning and memory neuroscientist at Oregon Health Sciences University in Portland, says, "Anything you learned two years ago is already old information. . . . Neuroscience is exploding" (Kotulak 1996, p. 124). In the coming years, we can expect new and more accurate technologies to further illuminate the brain's mysteries. For now, the following are the "workhorses" of neuroscience.

Brain Imaging Devices

Magnetic Resonance Imaging (MRI) machines provide high-quality cross-sectional images of soft tissue like the brain without X-rays or radiation. This tool has two new variations. Functional MRI (fMRI) is a lower budget variation, cheaper, and much faster. Another is NMRI (Nuclear Magnetic Resonance Imagery), which is 30,000 times faster and captures an image every 50 milliseconds. That speed allows us, for example, to measure the sequence of thinking across very narrow areas of the brain (see fig. 1.1).

FIGURE 1.1

Brain Imaging Technology
(Includes PET, fMRI, and CAT scans)

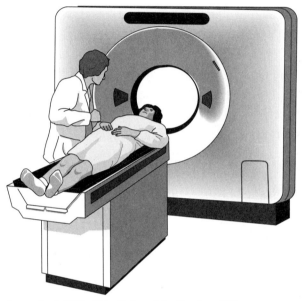

Animals

Lab experiments with rats, dogs, cats, slugs, apes, and other animals provide a rich source of information about how similar brains work. For example, we have learned much about the role of enriched environments from studying rat brains.

Computerized Electrodes

The electroencephalogram (EEG) gives us readings about the electrical output of the brain. Magneto-encephalography (MEG) uses high-tech sensors that are super-cooled, liquid-helium, and super-conductive to locate faint magnetic fields that are generated by the brain's neural networks. They've been used to detect brainwave patterns and abnormal cerebral functions such as seizures or dementia. These tools also can help us track, for example,

how much brain activity occurs during problem solving (see fig. 1.2).

Clinical Studies

We can learn much using human volunteers, often from university psychology classes. For example, flashing slides at high speeds can tell us about reaction times of the visual system. We've learned a great deal about what is "nature" and what is "nurture" from studies of twins.

PET

Positron Emission Tomography (PET) is an imaging device. The process of PET begins when a sub-

FIGURE 1.2

Common Electrode Placements for EEG
(Electroencephalogram)

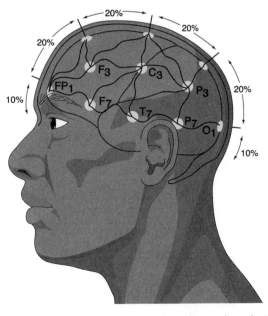

These readings give information about where in the brain electrical activity is taking place.

ject drinks some "spiked water" (O^{15}) or radioactive glucose. Then the PET reads the amount of radioactive substances released when certain areas of the brain consume glucose. If you were reading, for example, it would show glucose activity in the temporal and parietal lobes, with some in the occipital. (For a brief definition of any unfamiliar terms not defined in the text, please refer to the glossary on page 115.) A new variation on this tool, developed at the University of California at Los Angeles (UCLA), uses radioactive probes to hone in on genes specially "tagged" by researchers.

Autopsies

Weight, stages of development, and amount of decay or lesions can all be observed or measured by a neurological pathologist. Using autopsies, UCLA neuroscientist Bob Jacobs discovered that students with more challenging and demanding school lives had more dendritic branching than those who didn't. In other words, their brains had physically changed and were more enriched and complex.

Spectrometers

Ignored for decades, spectrometers are fast on the rise. These devices measure the specifics of brain chemicals, or neurotransmitters, as an activity occurs. For example, if I'm feeling depressed, it can tell me if there's been a change in the levels of specific neurotransmitters in my frontal lobes.

The Knowledge Explosion

During the '90s, brain research exploded into dozens of subdisciplines. Seemingly unrelated fields like genetics, physics, and pharmacology were seamlessly woven into scientific journal articles on the brain. Drawing from a body of technical knowledge about the brain, a whole new way of thinking about the organ developed. While we don't yet have an inclusive, coherent model of how the brain works, we do know enough to make significant changes in how we teach.

Primitive models on the workings of the brain have been around for 2,000 years. The brain has been referred to as a hydraulic system (the Greco-Roman model), a fluid system (Renaissance), an enchanted loom (the early Industrial Revolution), a city's switchboard (early to mid-1900s), and a computer (1950–1980s). Brain theory of the 1970s told us that we just needed more right-brained learning. Later, educators were introduced to the triune brain theory. This three-part evolutionary schema told us survival learning was in the lower brain, emotions were in the mid-brain, and higher-order thinking in the upper brain area. This model, first introduced in 1952, and popularized during the '70s and '80s, is now outdated. Today's educators should embrace a more complex "whole-systems approach" to understanding the brain. Much of this book will provide a more sound biological footing for this new interdisciplinary model grounded in brain research.

Before the "Decade of the Brain" ends, the '90s may be remembered as the emergence of the "chemical learner." Those with just the right "brain chemicals" (more or less serotonin, dopamine, or other related compounds) will succeed while those whose chemistry is not quite right will be inattentive, unmotivated, or violent. Brain-altering medications, mind food, and smart drugs already contribute to a billion-dollar, worldwide industry, and they may soon become the rule of the day. We see kids on Ritalin, dads on Prozac, and moms on Provera. Grandmothers are taking estrogen supplements to reduce the effects of Alzheimer's, and grandfathers are taking GM1 (ganglioside) or GDNF (glial-derived growth factor) to combat Parkinson's. It's a brave, new world, indeed.

Interpreting Brain Research

The military has a system for coding the level of certainty about surveillance information. At the weakest or lowest level you have unreliable sources, outdated information, and a lack of alternative confirming sources. At the other end of the spectrum is "high confidence." This means you have reliable original sources, fresh confirming sources, a variety of quality data gathering, and personal verification of data, perhaps even eyewitnesses.

Figure 1.3 demonstrates a similar classification system for interpreting brain research. At the lowest level of confidence, Level 1, is simple theory. There's nothing wrong with theory, as long as you recognize it for what it is. Level 2 means some discovery or experiment has illuminated the theory. It's better than Level 1, but it has a way to go. As a Level 2 example, consider neuroscientist Daniel Schacter's discovery that the brain stores real-life experiences differently than it does a fabricated story (1996). In medical experiments, PET scans revealed a visible difference in the brain between telling the truth and fabricated stories. Additional research to determine potential applications for this finding is necessary.

A Level 3 of confidence comes through widespread, documented clinical trials. Usually done at universities, these studies give us moderate levels

---

FIGURE 1.3

How to Interpret Brain Research

These levels are listed from most to least reliable, from top to bottom

Level 4: In-Context Applications

Done in schools or businesses, this documented action research gives us testing results under actual, real-life conditions.

Level 3: Clinical Studies

Usually university-supported, these studies are best with multiple experimenters, large, diverse, multi-age, multicultural populations (double-blind is preferable).

Level 2: Laboratory Discovery

Could come from autopsies, experiments, fMRI, PET, or EEG scans.

Level 1: Brain/Learning Theory

Any theory about learning and the brain that explains recurring behaviors.

---

of confidence in the research. Level 4 confidence means that action research, by you or other colleagues, has confirmed that the idea works across the board, for most anyone, most anywhere, reflecting a high confidence in the method. Most of the strategies described in this book will be at the higher end confidence levels (3–4 range).

Unfolding brain research is both exciting and full of pitfalls. The implications can be exhilarating, but it's just as important to consider the pitfalls. For example, educators can apply only a small percentage of brain research. Much of it is highly esoteric or disease oriented. Also, brain research doesn't necessarily "prove" anything. It merely suggests ideas or paths that have a higher probability of success. Nevertheless, a great deal of action research is necessary to advance our thinking. More important, we must not expect neuroscientists to present us with the "holy grail" to learning. Most paradigm-shaking breakthroughs have been an outside-the-box multidisciplinary insight.

While that news is old hat for some, it's a discouraging revelation for others. In fact, a great deal of what's useful and what's not will be uncovered by thoughtful educators like yourself who seriously turn to action research. We need more action research—not academic. As Frank Vellutino of the State University of New York at Albany observes, "We do more educational research than anyone else in the world, and we ignore more of it as well" (in Hancock 1996, p. 58).

Practical Suggestions

What's an educator to do with all this information? Three steps are indicated. First, become "consumer literate" in the field of brain research. Learn the major terms and the sources of research; decide who's credible and who isn't. Second, we need more action research, not learning theories. Begin in your own workplace. Start small and keep track of your results. Third, take this information to the public. Let your students in on what you're doing. Talk to parents about the brain, and make sure other staff members know about the information,

too. Get or give administrative backing. This helps generate the long-term resources and support needed for transformation.

Let's not jump to embrace any idea just because someone, somewhere has labeled it as "brain compatible." We all want solutions to educational challenges, but we must be careful about how we apply new discoveries. We've already gone through this in many areas. Howard Gardner's Theory of Multiple Intelligences has been used as "proof" for all kinds of things that he never proposed, said, or implied.

Your own questions ought to be, "From where did this idea originate? Is it still just theory? Where's the research on it?" You'll want to know, "What was the scientific discovery that illuminated the theory? What clinical trials have been done? Is there any evidence of successful applications in the classroom?" If you can get answers that satisfy you, then you are ahead of the "bandwagon" of educators who are still looking for some magic pill to solve their problems. The more you understand, the better you'll be able to decide what is and is not truly brain compatible.

Expect this book to help you sort the theories from the facts and the discoveries from the well-designed clinical trials. Use it as a study guide. Brain-compatible learning is here to stay. You can bet it will affect nearly everything we do including teaching strategies, discipline policies, the arts, special education, curriculum, technology, bilingual programs, music, learning environments, staff development, assessment, and even organizational change.

The Learning Brain

I f you wanted to get your car fixed, you'd likely go to a mechanic. For legal help, you'd find an attorney. To understand the brain and how we learn, would you go to a teacher? Probably not. Yet every year, millions of parents trust that the professionals who teach their children know something about the brain and processes of learning.

In defense of teachers, even neuroscientists still disagree on some of the inner workings of the brain. Most schools of education offer psychology, not neurology, courses. And these psychology courses, at best, provide indirect information about how children learn. Inservice training is directed at symptoms of problems not a working knowledge of the brain. Popular articles rarely offer the depth or point of view that today's educator needs.

Can we summarize the basics of how our brain learns? That's the goal of this chapter. Questions about the brain remain, but we know enough to help educators do a better job. By understanding how the brain learns, we can better allocate educational resources. Not only will we save money, but, more important, we will improve our successes with children.

The Human Brain

The adult human brain weighs about 3 pounds (1300–1400 grams). By comparison, a sperm whale brain weighs about 7800 grams, or 17 pounds! A dolphin brain weighs about 4 pounds and a gorilla brain about 1 pound. Your dog's brain weighs about 72 grams, which is only about 6 percent of your own brain's total weight.

Humans have large brains relative to body weight. Close to the size of a large grapefruit or cantaloupe, it's mostly water (78 percent), fat (10 percent), and protein (8 percent). A living brain is so soft it can be cut with a butter knife.

From the outside, the brain's most distinguishing features are its convolutions, or folds. These wrinkles are part of the cerebral cortex (Latin for "bark" or "rind"). The cerebral cortex is the orange-peel thick outer covering of the brain. The folds allow the covering to maximize surface area (more cells per square inch). In fact, if it were laid out, the cortex would be about the size of an unfolded single page from a daily newspaper. Yet it is only a grapefruit-sized organ. Its importance can be attributed to the fact that it makes up critical portions of the nervous system, and its nerve cells are connected by nearly 1 million miles of nerve fibers. The human brain has the largest area of uncommitted cortex (no specific function identified so far) of any species on earth (Howard 1994). This gives humans extraordinary flexibility for learning.

Taking Sides in Learning

We have two cerebral hemispheres, the left and the right. They are connected by bundles of nerve fibers, the largest known as the corpus callosum. The corpus callosum has about 250 million nerve fibers. Patients in whom it has been severed can still function in society. This interhemispheric freeway allows each side of the brain to exchange information more freely. While each side of the brain processes things differently, some earlier assumptions about the left and right brain are outdated.

In general, the left hemisphere processes things more in parts and sequentially. But musicians process music in their left hemisphere, not right as a novice would. Among left-handers, almost half use their right hemisphere for language. Higher-level mathematicians, problem solvers, and chess players have more right hemisphere activation during these tasks, while beginners in those activities usually are left-hemisphere active. For right-handers, gross motor function is controlled by the right hemisphere while fine motor is usually more of a left hemisphere activity. The right hemisphere recognizes negative emotions faster; the left hemisphere notices positive emotions faster (Ornstein and Sobel 1987). Studies indicate the left hemisphere is more active when we experience positive emotions. The importance of this information will become evident later in the book. But for now suffice it to say that the old biases about music and arts being "right-brained frills" are outdated (see fig. 2.1).

Scientists divide the brain into four areas called lobes, as illustrated in Figure 2.2. They are occipital, frontal, parietal, and temporal. The occipital lobe is in the middle back of the brain. It's primarily responsible for vision. The frontal lobe is the area around your forehead. It's involved with purposeful acts like judgment, creativity, problem solving, and planning. The parietal lobe is

FIGURE 2.1

Key Functional Areas of the Brain

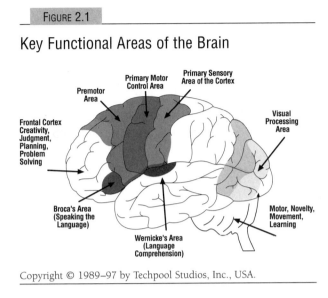

Copyright © 1989–97 by Techpool Studios, Inc., USA.

FIGURE 2.2

Lobes of the Brain

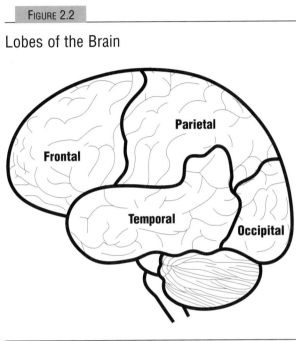

on the top back area. Its duties include processing higher sensory and language functions. The temporal lobes (left and right side) are above and around the ears. This area is primarily responsible for hearing, memory, meaning, and language. There is some overlap in the functions of the lobes.

The territory in the middle of the brain includes the hippocampus, thalamus, hypothalamus, and amygdala (see fig. 2.3). This mid-brain area (also known as the limbic system) represents 20 percent of the brain by volume, and is responsible for emotions, sleep, attention, body regulation, hormones, sexuality, smell, and production of most of the brain's chemicals. However, others say there is no "limbic" system, only specific structures that process emotion, like the amygdala (LeDoux 1996 pp. 97–100). Still others, like Paul MacLean, disagree and still call the middle of the brain "the limbic (or emotional) area" (1990).

The location of the brain area that allows you to know that you are "you" (consciousness) is dis-

puted. It might be dispersed throughout the cortex, in the thalamus, or it may be located near the reticular formation atop the brain stem. Much of the cerebrum, which makes up 75 percent of the total volume, has no yet identified single purpose and is often referred to as the "association cortex." Gray neurons or cell bodies form the cerebral cortex and other nuclei. The white in the brain is the myelin sheath that coats the connective fibers (axons).

The sensory cortex (monitoring your skin receptors) and the motor cortex (needed for movement) are narrow bands across the top middle of the brain. In the back lower area of the brain is the cerebellum (Latin for "little brain"), which is primarily responsible for balance, posture, motor movement, and some areas of cognition (see fig. 2.3). Recent experiments strongly support the con-

FIGURE 2.3

Medial View of the Brain

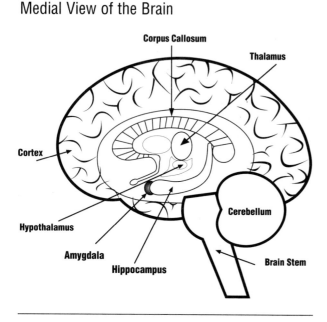

clusion that essential long-term memory traces for motor learning are located in the cerebellum (Thompson 1993).

Energy for Learning

The brain is energy inefficient. It is about 2 percent of the body's adult weight, but it consumes about 20 percent of the body's energy. How does the brain get its energy to learn? Its primary source is blood, which supplies nutrients like glucose, protein, trace elements, and oxygen. The brain gets about 8 gallons of blood each hour, about 198 gallons per day. In addition, water provides the electrolytic balance for proper functioning. The brain needs 8 to 12 glasses of water a day for optimal functioning. Dehydration is a common problem in school classrooms, leading to lethargy and impaired learning (Hannaford 1995). The role of nutrition will be

explored in the next chapter, but for the moment we can say that good diets do help learning.

Oxygen is, of course, critical to the brain. The brain uses one fifth of the body's oxygen. If the blood supply to the brain is interrupted, we lose consciousness in seconds. Fortunately, the brain usually gets enough oxygen for basic functioning because the carotid artery ensures the brain gets freshly oxygenated blood first after leaving the heart-lung area. Higher levels of attention, mental functioning, and healing are linked to better quality air (less carbon dioxide, more oxygen). Many of the so-called "smart drugs" that boost alertness, cognitive functioning, and memory enhance oxygen flow to the brain. With only 36 percent of K–12 students in a daily physical education class, are they getting enough of the oxygen-rich blood needed for highest performance? Many worry that they are not.

Where Learning Begins

There are two kinds of brain cells: neurons and glia. While the majority of brain cells (90 percent) are glia, it is the remaining 10 percent—the neurons—are much better understood. The most studied brain cells are neurons (Greek for "bowstring"). For the sake of comparison, a fruit fly has 100,000 neurons, a mouse has 5 million, and a monkey has 10 billion. You have about 100 billion neurons. Healthy adults have the same number of neurons as found in the brain of a 2-year-old. A single cubic millimeter (1/16,000th of an inch) of brain tissue has more than 1 million neurons. They are about 50 microns in diameter. You lose your brain cells every day through attrition, decay, and disuse. Scientists differ on exactly how many; estimates vary from 10,000 to 100,000 per day (Howard 1994). You've got enough for your lifetime, though. Even if you lost a half million neurons per day, it would take centuries to, literally, lose your mind.

The most numerous of your brain's cells are called interneurons, or glial (Greek for "glue"). They have no cell body. You have about 1,000 billion of them. The role of glial cells may include formation of the blood-brain barrier, transport of nutrients, and regulation of the immune system. They also remove dead cells and give structural support that improves firmness (see fig. 2.4).

Though the brain contains fewer neurons, they are essential to performing the brain's work.

Neurons consist of a compact cell body, dendrites, and axons (see fig. 2.5). They are responsible for information processing, and converting chemical and electrical signals back and forth. Two things are critical about a neuron when compared with other cells in the body. First, new research at Salk Institute in La Jolla, California, reveals that some areas of the brain can and do grow new neurons (Kempermann, Kuhn, and Gage 1997). Second, a normal functioning neuron is continuously firing, integrating, and generating information; it's a virtual hotbed of activity.

Although the cell body has the capacity to move, most adult neurons stay put; they simply

---

FIGURE 2.4

Common Types of Glial Cells

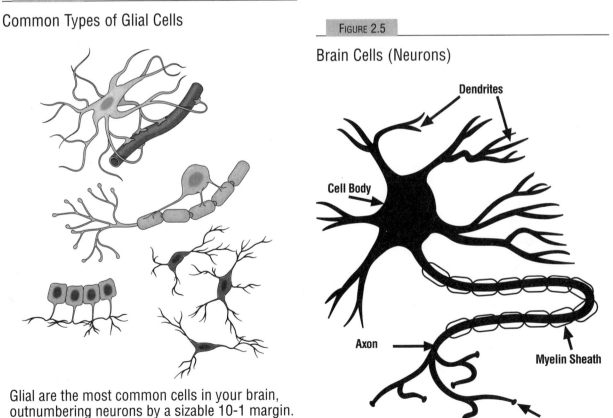

Glial are the most common cells in your brain, outnumbering neurons by a sizable 10-1 margin.

FIGURE 2.5

Brain Cells (Neurons)

Dendrites

Cell Body

Axon

Myelin Sheath

Axon Terminals

extend axons outward. While many dendrites, or fibers, may extend from a neuron, each has only one axon. The axon is a thinner, leg-like extension that connects with other dendrites. Most axons only connect with dendrites; normally, dendrites don't connect with one another. To connect with thousands of other cells, the axon splits to subdivide itself and branches in two, over and over again. Neurons only serve to pass along information; none of them is just a receiver alone or the end of the connection. Information flows in one direction only; at the neuronal level, it's always going *from* the cell body down the axon to the synapse. It never goes from the tip of the axon back up to a cell body.

The axon has two essential functions: to conduct information in the form of electrical stimulation and to transport chemical substances. The longest axons (running down a spinal cord) may be up to a meter long, but most are closer to a centimeter. The thicker the axon, the faster it conducts electricity and information. Myelin is a fatty substance that forms around well-used axons, and all of the larger axons are myelinated. This seems not only to speed up the electrical transmission (up to 12-fold), but it also reduces interference from other nearby reactions. Nodes along the axons, along with myelination, can boost electrical impulses to speeds of 120 meters per second, or 200 miles an hour. The shortest axons probably have no advantage in being myelinated; it would be like having a speedy carpool lane for only a half-mile stretch.

No neuron is an end point or termination for information; it only serves to pass it on. A single neuron can receive signals from thousands of other cells, sometimes as far as a meter away, and its axon can branch repeatedly, sending signals to thousands more. But, in general, neurons connect most with other close-by neurons. More connections makes for more efficient communications. Just as city traffic can develop bottlenecks, alternative routes can provide an escape valve. The sum total of all the synaptic reactions arriving from all the dendrites to the cell body at any moment will determine whether that cell, will in fact, fire itself. If enough arriving signals stimulate the neuron, it will fire. Dendrites are branch-like extensions that grow outward from the cell body when the environment is enriched. Information is carried inside a neuron by electrical pulses and is transmitted across the synaptic gap from one neuron to another by chemicals called neurotransmitters (see fig. 2.6). Learning is a critical function of neurons

FIGURE 2.6

How Neurons Make Connections:
Axon-Synapse-Dendrite Pathways Are Electrical to Chemical to Electrical

that cannot be accomplished individually—it requires groups of neurons (Greenfield 1995).

How Do We Learn?

What the human brain does best is learn. Learning changes the brain because it can rewire itself with each new stimulation, experience, and behavior. Scientists are unsure precisely *how* this happens, but they have some ideas *what* happens.

First, some kind of stimulus to the brain starts the process. It could be internal (a brainstorm!) or it could be a new experience, like solving a jigsaw puzzle. Then, the stimulus is sorted and processed at several levels. Finally, there's the formation of a memory potential. That simply means the pieces are in place so that the memory can be easily activated. As educators, it's well worth our time to understand the basics of these. It may give us some useful insights into how students learn.

The Stimulus

To our brain, we are either doing something we already know how to do or we are doing something new. If we are repeating an earlier learning, there's a good chance the neural pathways will become more and more efficient. They do that through myelination, which, as noted earlier, is the process of adding a fatty coating to axons. Once myelination has occurred, the brain gets more efficient. Washington University School of Medicine researchers Hanneke Van Mier and Steve Peterson discovered that while many areas of the brain will "light up" on a PET scan when a new task is initiated, the brain "lights up" less and is used less the better the task is learned. Novices use more of their brain, but they are less efficient at how they use it. This quality illustrates how quickly our brain adapts and rewires itself.

While exercise is doing what we already know how to do, *stimulation* is doing something new. Seeing a new movie, listening to new music, singing a new song, visiting a new place, solving a new problem, or making new friends can all stimulate the brain. As long as it's coherent, this novel mental or motor stimulation produces greater beneficial electrical energy than the old-hat stuff. This input is converted to nervous impulses. They travel to extraction and sorting stations like the thalamus, located in the middle of the brain. In intentional behavior, a multisensory convergence takes place and the "map" is quickly formed in the hippocampus (Freeman 1995). From there, signals are distributed to specific areas of the brain.

Once this input is received, each brain cell acts as a tiny electrical battery. It's powered by the difference in concentration of sodium and potassium ions across a cell membrane. Changes in voltage help power the transmitting of signals for dendritic growth. Neurotransmitters are stored in the ends of the cell's axon, which nearly touches the dendrites of another cell. Typically, they'll either be excitatory (like glutamate) or inhibitory (like GABA, or gamma-aminobutyric acid). When the cell body sends an electrical discharge outward to the axon, it stimulates the release of those stored chemicals into the synaptic gap, which is the space between the end of an axon and tip of a dendrite, as represented in Figure 2.7.

Once in that gap, the chemical reaction triggers (or inhibits) new electrical energy in the receptors of the contacted dendrite. It's electrical to chemical and back to electrical. There, the process is repeated to the next cell. Eventually, the repeated electrical stimulation fosters, along with an increased input of

FIGURE 2.7

Learning Takes Place at the Synapse

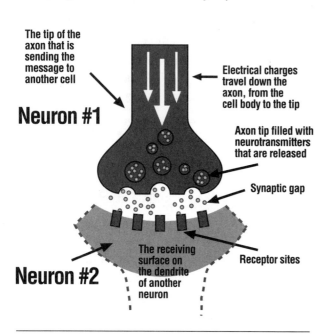

The tip of the axon that is sending the message to another cell

Neuron #1

Electrical charges travel down the axon, from the cell body to the tip

Axon tip filled with neurotransmitters that are released

Synaptic gap

Receptor sites

The receiving surface on the dendrite of another neuron

Neuron #2

nutrients, cell growth by way of dendritic branching. These branches help us make even more connections until, in some cases, whole "neural forests" help us understand better and, maybe someday, make us an expert in that topic. When we say cells "connect" with other cells, we really mean that they are in such close proximity that the synapse is easily, and almost effortlessly, "used" over and over again. New synapses usually appear after learning.

The Formation of Lasting Learning

Learning and memory are two sides of a coin to neuroscientists. You can't talk about one without the other. After all, if you have learned something, the only evidence of the learning is memory. Unfortunately, this final part of the learning process has proved to be an enormous and frustrating challenge for scientists. Just when they think they've figured it out, they discover it's more like a house of mirrors. In short, they're still looking for answers.

Donald Hebb, the great Canadian psychologist, correctly postulated more than 50 years ago that learning occurs when a cell requires *less* input from another cell the next time it's activated. In other words, it has "learned" to respond differently. More recently, a research team at MIT lead by Nobel laureates Susumu Tonegawa and Eric Kandel has identified a single, specific gene that activates this critical memory formation (Saltus 1997). This breakthrough may explain why some people have a better memory than others: It's partly gene controlled.

Lasting learning, or long-term potentiation (LTP), has tentatively been accepted as essential to the actual physical process of learning. Since its discovery in 1973 by Bliss and Lomo, countless experiments have defined its intricacies. Briefly, here's the process.

A cell is electrically stimulated over and over so that it excites a nearby cell. If a weaker stimulus is then applied to the neighboring cell a short time later, the cell's ability to get excited is enhanced. Neural activity can have either an excitatory or inhibitory effect. Suppressing an inhibitory process can result in its activation. Another effect helps us learn too. LTD (long-term depression) occurs when a synapse is altered so that it is *less* likely to fire. By making the wrong connection less likely, quicker learning is promoted. This occurs when we do trial-and-error learning (Siegfried 1997). In other words, cells change their receptivity to messages based on previous stimulation. That sounds like the cells have "learned" and changed their behavior. In short, our learning is done through the alteration of synaptic efficacy.

Learning and Behavior

While it's exciting to make some sense out of the actual cell-to-cell connections, learning and behavior are often different. You might have learned how to teach a better class from a book. But your behavior might still be the same as it has always been. Why and how does this happen? Certainly, we could point to outside circumstances like excess stress or a student's behavior. Yet our behaviors are more likely governed by our complex emotional states and memories. The daily chemistry of our brain adds great complexity to the question, "How does our brain learn?"

Our everyday behaviors are heavily affected by other "floating" chemicals in the brain: the monoamines and peptides. In fact, one researcher estimates that over 98 percent of all your brain's and body's internal communications are through peptides, not synapses (Pert 1997, p. 139). If the neurotransmitters we mentioned earlier, like glutamate and GABA, act as "cellular phones" offering specific communications, the other chemicals act more like huge bullhorns that can broadcast to wide areas of the brain. These chemicals are usually serotonin, dopamine, and noradrenaline. These produce the behaviors that you can actually see in class like attention, stress, or drowsiness. Later chapters will address these further. In short, learning happens on many complex layers at once, from the cellular to the behavioral.

Getting Smarter

The end result of learning for humans is intelligence. Regardless of how you define intelligences, having a bigger brain or more brain cells per cubic inch doesn't help. A dolphin has a bigger brain, and a rat brain has more cell density than a human brain. The key to getting smarter is growing more synaptic connections between brain cells and not losing existing connections. It's the connections that allow us to solve problems and figure things out.

What percentage of your physical brain do you use? On a given day, most areas are used because functions are well distributed throughout it. In addition, it has been customizing itself for your lifestyle since the day you were born. It generally works well for you because you've encouraged it to develop for your precise world. If you're good at music, you're likely to sing, compose, or play. If you're good at sports, you're likely to practice or play. If you're good at numbers, you're likely to do some computation daily. In the real world, your brain's just right for you.

On a more theoretical, mathematical basis, the story is much different. It is estimated that we use less than 1 percent of 1 percent of our brain's projected processing capacity. Each of your 100 billion neurons ordinarily connects with 1,000–10,000 other neurons. But they could theoretically connect with far more. Since each neuron has several thousand synapses, your entire brain has trillions of them. Your brain is capable of processing as much as 10^{27} bits of data per second (Hobson 1994). However, Paul Churchland (1995) postulates that the total possible configuration is 10 to the 100 trillionth power. That number far exceeds the number of known particles in the universe. Our brain is, indeed, quite a miracle. The brain is what we have; the mind is what it does. In other words, the "mind" is not a thing; it's a process.

Could this potential neural connectivity be responsible for so-called "genius" behavior in isolated individuals? We don't know yet. Almost 10 percent of children under 5 have a photographic memory as do 1 percent of adults. Savants can calculate huge numbers and, in some cases, do it as fast as a computer. There are documented cases where subjects have spoken a dozen or more languages, demonstrated thought transference, performed speed reading, or showcased a super-memory. Others have shown us extraordinary use of ESP, remote viewing, or early musical gifts (Murphy 1992). Could these become commonplace in our classrooms? Could we engineer the development of another Albert Einstein, Maya Angelou, Amadeus Mozart, Martha Graham, or Bill Gates?

Finally, if learning is what we value, then we ought to value the process of learning as much as the result of learning. Our brain is highly effective and adaptive. What ensures our survival is adapting and creating options. A typical classroom narrows our thinking strategies and answer options. Educators who insist on singular approaches and the "right answer" are ignoring what's kept our species around for centuries. Humans have survived for thousands of years by trying out new things, *not* by always getting the "right," tried-and-true answer. That's not healthy for growing a smart, adaptive brain. The notion of narrowed standardized tests to get the right answer violates the law of adaptiveness in a developing brain. Good quality education encourages the exploration of alternative thinking, multiple answers, and creative insights.

So what do we do about this brain knowledge? Is it useless theory? Not for the professional educator. As long as we are in "the business of learning," the brain is relevant. We have finally learned enough to formulate some important action steps. Many areas require more research, but dozens of studies are clear and solid enough to be transformed into classroom practice. Share with your students how their brains learn and work. Talk to interested parents about it, too. Many solutions to everyday problems will be presented in the upcoming chapters. But be prepared: There also will be many questions.

3 Getting Students Ready to Learn

Educators continually complain that students are not ready to learn. They show up for school underfed or malnourished, angry or apathetic, stressed, threatened, and sleepy. If they have been assigned homework, it's often not done. Naturally, this makes the roles of both teacher and learner much more difficult. It seems that schools must make a choice: leave it up to students to be ready to learn when they walk in the door, or become a "surrogate family," helping children to prepare to learn each day. This chapter considers how educators and parents can and might better manage the influences that prepare children's minds and brains for school.

Are Kids Really Different Now?

It's common to hear experienced teachers talk about "how kids used to be." But are children's brains really any different today than they were 30 or 40 years ago? We don't know for sure. No one has saved a variety of brains to compare, and today's technology was unavailable back then (see fig. 3.1).

FIGURE 3.1

Are Kids Today Biologically Different Than They Were 30 Years Ago?

Fewer natural foods and
more additives

More children raised in
single parent households
with fewer resources

More exposure to drugs
and medications

More exposure to passive
babysitters and sedentary
entertainment like TV

Use of car seats and seat belts
restricts movement but is safer

Less early motor
stimulation from
swings, see-saws,
merry-go-rounds, and
playground games because
of safety and liability concerns

Interestingly, there is some evidence that children today really are less prepared for school than they were one or two generations ago (Healy 1990, pp. 13–46). If you're wondering why children seem more violent, stressed, scattered, unfocused, and overall less ready for school, you're not alone. Many scientists agree with you—for example, Craig Ramey from the University of Alabama and Christopher Coe of the University of Wisconsin. The evidence can be seen in many critical areas, including emotional development, motor-sensory development, and school-day readiness.

School Readiness Starts at Conception

The first opportunity to get children ready for school is in the womb. We know that drugs, smoking, nutrition, and heredity all affect the embryo (Van Dyke and Fox 1990). The most important things a pregnant woman can do are eat well, avoid drugs, and keep the stress down.

A developing fetus is very sensitive to stress and poor nutrition. Most brain cells are produced between the fourth and seventh month of gestation. Those fast-developing cells, called neurons, form a vast network, connecting to other cells. A newborn has more than a trillion connections in the brain.

The developing brain grows so fast, counting brain cells is hopeless (though fig. 3.2 attempts to illustrate the rate of growth). Neurobiologist Peter Huttenlocher of the University of Chicago says it's like counting snowflakes in a blizzard or drops of water in a torrential rainstorm. At its peak, the embryo is generating brain cells at the rate of 250,000 a minute, or 15 million cells per hour. If

you knew your brain was being shaped at that rate, would you be cautious about what you did to it? Some parents are not careful, and we must work with their children in school every day.

Emotional Intelligence Begins Early

The book *Emotional Intelligence* (Goleman 1995) brought to public attention the importance of our emotional lives. But when does emotional intelligence develop, and is it too late to cultivate it by the time children arrive at school? The evidence suggests that emotional intelligence develops early, and the school years may be a time of last resort for nurturing emotional literacy.

An infant's relationship with its primary caretaker often determines whether the child develops learning problems. Harold Rubenstein of the Dartmouth Medical School says that troubled early relationships cause the child's brain to consume glucose in dealing with stress, glucose that instead could be used for early cognitive functions. Early exposure to stress or violence also causes the brain to reorganize itself, increasing receptor sites for alertness chemicals (Kotulak 1996). This increases reactivity and blood pressure, and the child will be more impulsive and aggressive in school.

Much of our emotional intelligence is learned in the first year. Children learn how to react in hundreds of simple cause-and-effect situations with parents. These situations guide them about being disappointed, pleased, anxious, sad, fearful, proud, ashamed, delighted, or apologetic. Children need this close, connected interaction and handling (Wilson, Willner, Kurz, and Nadel 1986). Known as "attunement," this process must happen during the critical first year of role modeling or children

FIGURE 3.2

Rapid Pace of Prenatal Brain Development

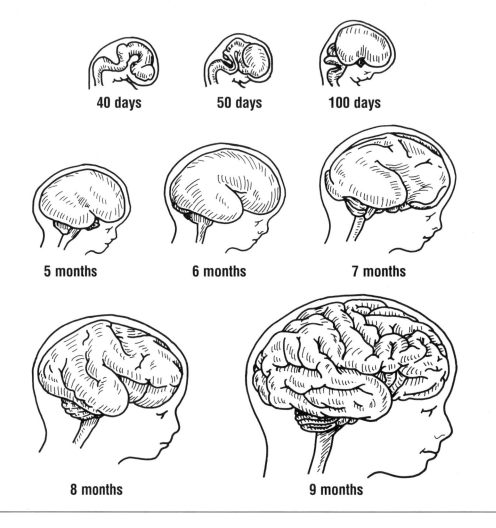

may end up emotionally corrupt. Even a parent's gestures are important (Thal, Tobias, and Morrison 1991). "This is when the primary caregiver plays back the proper and critical emotional responses," says psychiatrist Daniel Stern (Begley 1996).

We now understand that the first 48 months of life are critical to the brain's development. While researchers have always known that infant development was important, they never knew just *how* important. Wayne State neurobiologist Harry Chugani says the experiences of the first year "can completely change the way a person turns out" (Kotulak 1996, p. 46). But more often than not in today's world, the first few years are spent in a child-care center. Typical ratios of infants and toddlers to caregivers are from 3-1 up to 12-1. If parents understood the developmental opportunities in the infant's brain during those months, they might change their decision about who's minding their baby.

How much temperament is learned and how much is inherited? Harvard psychologist Jerome Kagan has studied infants extensively and says it's about half and half. The genetic part of our behavior is governed from our developing mid-brain area. "The physiological data implicate inherited variation in the excitability of the amygdala and its projections as one basis for the contrasting styles," says J.M. Kagan (1994, pp. 35, 171). But the first 24 months of child-raising provides the difference between several dramatically different and possible futures. For example, parents who recognize appropriate risk taking and acknowledge it will usually get a more courageous child. Parents who are fearful will communicate that by placing limitations on crawling or walking (Kagan 1994).

Preparing the Early Brain

Do today's children get the necessary stimulation for school readiness? "Not usually," says Lyelle Palmer, professor of special education at Winona State University in Minnesota. "The human brain is the most responsive organ you could imagine. But even with a universe of learning potential awaiting us, we usually don't even get around to doing the basics" (1997).

The brain is literally customizing itself for your particular lifestyle from the day you're born. Soon after, the brain prunes away unneeded cells and billions of unused connections. It's a time of enor-

mous selective receptiveness. The question is, "For what are you customizing your brain?" For educators, the question is even more pointed, "Exactly what talents, abilities, and experiences are students being exposed to and, on the other hand, what are they missing out on?" Here are a few examples.

The Motor Brain

Most educators know the value of "crawl time" in developing learning readiness. Yet many of today's children don't get the early motor stimulation needed for basic, much less optimal, school success. Today's infant is "baby-sat" by television, seated in a walker, or strapped in a car seat for hundreds of precious motor development hours. In 1960, the average 2-year-old spent an estimated 200 hours in a car. Today's 2-year-old has spent an estimated 500 hours in a car seat!

While infant safety is vital, few parents ever compensate for the confined, strapped-in hours. Considering the tomes of evidence on the impact of early motor stimulation on reading, writing, and attentional skills (Ayers 1972, 1991; Hannaford 1995), it's no wonder many children have reading problems. Although research on the general value of motor skills first surfaced many years ago, only today do we know about the specific value in reading, stress response, writing, attention, memory, and sensory development. As an example, the inner ear's vestibular area plays a key role in school readiness. Restak (1979) says, "Infants who were given periodic vestibular stimulation by rocking gain weight faster, develop vision and hearing earlier." Many link the lack of vestibular stimulation to dozens of learning problems including dyslexia (Cleeland 1984). How important is the timing of motor development? Felton Earls of the Harvard

Medical School says, "A kind of irreversibility sets in. . . . By age four you have essentially designed a brain that is not going to change very much more" (Kotulak 1996, p. 7). And while much learning happens after age four, much of the brain's infrastructure is now in place.

The Visual Brain

Neurobiologists tell us that much of our vision develops in our first year, particularly in the first 4 to 6 months, with a major growth spurt at age 2 to 4 months. This window is much earlier than previous studies indicated. With more than 30 distinct visual areas in the brain (including color, movement, hue, and depth), the growing infant must get a variety of stimulating input, including plenty of practice handling objects and learning their shapes, weight, and movement. A variety of objects, games, and responses from parents shape the way vision develops very early. "Children need a flood of information, a banquet, a feast," says neuroscientist Martha Pierson of the Baylor College of Medicine (in Kotulak 1996).

The "flood" should not come from television, which often is used as a baby-sitter (Tonge 1990). Television provides no time for reflection, interactions, or three-dimensional visual development. Parents would be wise to invest the time talking to their babies, speaking in short sentences and pointing out objects that are here and now, or three dimensional.

Television is two dimensional, and the developing brain needs depth, says V.L. Ramachandran, a neuroscientist and vision specialist at the University of California at San Diego. Television moves fast and talks about abstractions that are often nonexistent in the child's environment. It allows the eyes

no time to relax. This stress can aggravate learning difficulties. Television is a poor replacement for sensory-motor development time and key relationship time. The exposure to violence and a too-fast vocabulary takes a toll (Healy 1990, Strasburger 1992). Many scientists and researchers say they would ban television for all children before age 8 (Hannaford 1995). This gives the brain time to better develop its language, social, and motor skills.

Early Thinking Skills

The brain is fully ready for thinking through tactile learning as early as nine months. The cortex is not fully developed yet, but the cerebellum is ready. This cauliflower-shaped organ at the back bottom of the brain works overtime in infants. And some researchers suggest that it is very sophisticated in its learning capacity (Greenfield 1995). Intriguing studies suggest infants may understand basic counting principles and simple physics before age 1. Neural circuits for math and logic are ready for "planting the seeds" at this age. Some have shown (Wynn 1992) that infants can learn simple math long before their brains are ready for abstraction. Even if infants can do only a fraction of what they seem to be "wired" to do, it's a great deal. Parents who explore these possibilities are laying the foundation for long-term success in school.

The Auditory Brain

Patricia Kuhl of the University of Washington (Begley 1996) says that infants develop in their first year a perceptual map of responsive neurons in the auditory cortex. Circuits in the auditory cortex allocate both cells and receptor sites for what are quickly deemed the early survival sounds. This map is formed by hearing early sounds, and accents and word pronunciations are a big part of it. These phonemes alert infants to the particular inflections like a Spanish rolled "r" or a sharp Japanese "Hi!" As a result, the brain dedicates special neurons to be receptive to those particular sounds.

This developing map is so customized for the household that children are "functionally deaf" to sounds outside of their home environments. The greater the early vocabulary children are exposed to, the better. All of the early sounds shape the brain, even music and rhythm. In fact, research at the University of California at Irvine suggests that infants are quite receptive to and discerning about music. Since math and music circuitry are related, introducing music at this age may assist math later on (Weinberger 1994).

Language Development

Rutgers University neuroscientist and language specialist Paula Tallal says, "Language problems in children are associated with stressful pregnancies." "Not only can the sex hormone go awry during this time," she continues, "but other compounds, such as stress hormones, can be raised to abnormal levels." That's because the release or inhibition of hormones changes hemispheric development. She adds, "Having a stressful pregnancy is highly correlated with the failure to show the expected structural lateralization" (in Kotulak 1993, Section 1, p. 4). As a result, you often get stuttering and dyslexia in the child. The left side of the brain processes rapid auditory information faster than the right. That skill is critical in separating the sounds of speech into distinct units for comprehension. The left hemisphere, usually responsible for language development, develops slower in the male brain. Thus, males usually develop more language problems than females.

Infants whose parents talk to them more frequently and use bigger, "adult" words will develop better language skills, says Janellen Huttenlocher at the University of Chicago (in Kotulak 1993, Section 1, p. 4). "During this time, there is a huge vocabulary to be acquired." This crucial time lays the pathway for reading skills later on (Begley 1996, p. 57). Unfortunately, many parents still don't know how important it is to read to their children. A recent poll showed that 82 percent of all parents say they don't encourage reading at home ("Reading at Home" 1996). Worse yet, three out of four adults say kids are "too distracted" by television to read. Another survey reports that 90 percent of children age 9–13 play video games ("Video Games" 1996). While 43 percent play under an hour a day, 27 percent play 2 to 6 hours a day.

Developing reading skills is another story. Although babies can learn to see, point to, and say a word, there's little meaning until they have sufficient life experience to match words and experience. Studies suggest babies listen to words even though they cannot yet speak. All the words, understood or not, are contributing to the development of syntax, vocabulary, and meaning. It is believed that this time is critical for language development. Surprisingly, there is no absolute timetable for learning to read. Differences of three years *are* normal. Some children will be ready to read at 4 years; others, just as normal, will be ready at 7 or even 10 years. The child who reads at 7 might not be "developmentally delayed" as many have diagnosed. J.M. Kagan talks about how different infants can be even when they're just months old. "I have not seen an infant who was aroused by *every* type of event: some were excited by moving sights but not by sounds, and others showed the reverse profile" (1994, p. 39). Is whole language or direct phonics instruction more brain compatible? Research suggests there is value in each; a combination is best.

The Sudbury Valley School in Framingham, Massachusetts, is an example of a school that understands how reading readiness and the differences in learners' brains can coexist. Their K-12 program does not force reading on any student. They believe that youngsters are already exposed to thousands of vocabulary words in the world. Instead of teaching them reading, the school simply lets students choose to do it when they are ready. As a result, some children read at age 5, others at 6, some as late as 10. But according to the school's founder, Daniel Greenberg, the school has 100 percent truly functional, literate graduates. There are no reading disorders or dyslexia, and everyone likes to read. It's an approach that says, "Wait until the brain's ready to read, then you can't stop it!" (Greenberg 1991).

Sweet Dreams

Teachers often complain about kids falling asleep in school. Is it the parent's fault or the school's? Studies asking why kids seem to fall asleep so often in middle and high school classes have now turned to biology. Researchers had already looked at two possible culprits that, in the end, didn't seem to matter much: part-time work and going to bed late. The answer wasn't social pressure, either. It was puberty.

Sleep is regulated by many chemicals, including amines, glutocorticoids, and oleamide, a drowsiness-inducing chemical substance, says Dale Boger, a molecular biologist at Scripps Research Institute in La Jolla, California. A delayed accumulation of oleamide means a teen's natural sleep clock generates a natural bedtime closer to midnight with a waking time closer to 8 a.m. This

change is believed to be stimulated by the hormonal changes of puberty. Sleep expert Mary Carskadon, formerly of Brown University, confirms that most teenagers are affected by this critical biological change in their internal sleep clocks (in Viadero 1995). "We have kids so sleep-deprived, it's almost as if they're drugged. Educators like myself are teaching walking zombies," says Cornell University sleep disorder expert James Maas (in L. Richardson 1996, p. E-1). Sleep experts discovered that teens simply couldn't fall asleep early, as their frustrated parents suggested. Carskadon calls it a "delayed phase preference," and the body's changing chemistry is the culprit. While many researchers are unsure of the direct cause, the results are easy to see. They should be able to get to sleep earlier, but they can't. It's like the biological clock injected amphetamines into the brain. Milton Erman, professor at the University of California in San Diego, says, "High school kids are grossly sleep deprived. . . . [I]t makes very little scientific sense to make these kids function at these very early hours" (in L. Richardson 1996, p. E-1). Richard Allen of the Sleep Disorder Center at Johns Hopkins University studied two groups of teens. The later risers performed better academically. One started school at 7:30 a.m., the other at 9:30 a.m.

Researchers have discovered that at night, the first few minutes and the last few minutes of our four-part sleep cycle take us into a theta state. That's our own "twilight zone," when we are half awake and half asleep. Brain wave cycles here are about 4–7 per minute as we drift randomly in and out of sleep. Ordinarily, our waking hours are spent in alpha and beta time, from 8–25 cycles per second. During theta state, we can be awakened easily and often rehash the day or think of things we have to do the next day. This light sleep stage usually consumes only about 5 percent of our night. It usually occurs upon awakening and at bedtime. This drowsy, or deep reverie, is a mildly altered state of consciousness, good for free associating.

The heavier, nondream states of sleep are important for physical renewal. During our "dead to the world" states, the pituitary gland delivers extra growth and repair hormones to the bloodstream. This helps rebuild tissue and ensure our immune system is in order. During this state, you rarely hear a noise in your house unless it's almost an explosion. This rest and repair period is the majority of our sleep time. Theta usually lasts less than 5 percent, dream time 25 percent, and our delta ("deep sleep") state is the remainder.

The critical time in question is the dream state, or rapid eye movement (REM) time. This state is thought to be critical to maintaining our memories (Hobson 1994). A highly active area during REM time is the amygdala, a structure known to be crucial for processing intense emotions. In addition, the entorhinal cortex, known to be critical in long-term memory processing, also is active (Ackerman 1996). Bruce McNaughton at the University of Arizona discovered that a rat's brain activity patterns in REM match the patterns of the daytime learning session (Lasley 1997). He suggests that during sleep time, the hippocampus is rehearsing the learning sent to it by the neocortex. This "instant replay" consolidates and enhances memory. That may be why waking up too early affects this all-important REM sleep. Of all the time to sleep, we need those last few hours the most.

Both Carskadon (Viadero 1995) and Carey (1991) suggest a solution. Middle and high schools ought to start later than elementary school. While 7:30 a.m. is appropriate for the primary levels, a 9:30 a.m. start usually works better for middle and high schools. In Corpus Christi, Texas, a district-wide change to later start times resulted in better learning, fewer sleeping-at-school teens, and fewer discipline problems. It makes sense: If we want kids to learn and remember, they'll need to stay awake at school and get enough sleep time to consolidate the learning at night.

Eating to Learn

Many school food-service programs were designed for bone and muscle growth, not the brain's learning requirements. There can be a middle ground. Food must supply the nutrients necessary for learning, and the critical nutrients include proteins, unsaturated fats, vegetables, complex carbohydrates, and sugars. The brain also needs a wide range of trace elements such as boron, selenium, vanadium, and potassium.

The National Research Council publishes an annual report on nutrition, and the findings have been summarized by many (Woteki and Thomas 1992). The report concludes that Americans eat too much saturated fat, sugar, and simple carbohydrates. They eat too few fruits, vegetables, and complex carbohydrates. Even with federally funded breakfast programs, many kids still get only simple carbohydrates. That's insufficient for basic, much less optimal, learning and memory (Wurtman 1986). In addition, many children have food allergies (most commonly to dairy products) that can cause behavioral and learning problems (Gislason 1996).

Are specific foods particularly good for the brain? There are many, but children rarely get enough of them. They include leafy green vegetables, salmon, nuts, lean meats, and fresh fruits (Connors 1989). Other evidence indicates that vitamin and mineral supplements can boost learning, memory, and intelligence (Ostrander and Schroeder 1991, Hutchinson 1994). Calpain has been found to act as a "cleaner" for synapses, dissolving protein buildup (Howard 1994). This makes them more efficient for neural transmission, hence learning. The dietary source for calpain is dairy products (yogurt and milk are best) and leafy green vegetables (spinach and kale are excellent). Most kids eat to get rid of their hunger and lack sufficient information to eat for optimal learning. This is a concern because the essential myelination and maturation of the brain is going full speed up to 25 years of age.

Drinking to Learn

Dehydration is a common problem that's linked to poor learning. To be at their best, learners need water. When we are thirsty, it's because there's a drop in the water content of the blood. When the water percentage in the blood drops, the salt concentration in the blood is higher. Higher salt levels increase the release of fluids from the cells into the bloodstream (Ornstein and Sobel 1987). That raises blood pressure and stress. Stress researchers found that within five minutes of drinking water, there is a marked decline in corticoids and ACTH, two hormones associated with elevated stress (Heybach and Vernikos-Danellis 1979). In addition, if water is available in the learning environment, the typical hormone response to the stress (elevated levels of corticoids) is "markedly reduced or absent" (Levine and Coe 1989). These studies suggest a strong role for water in keeping learners' stress levels in check.

Because the brain is made up of a higher percentage of water than any other organ, dehydration takes a toll quickly. There's a loss of attentiveness,

and lethargy sets in. Dehydration means many children need more water, more often. Soft drinks, juice, coffee, or tea are diuretics that don't help much. Teachers should encourage students to drink water throughout the day. Parents who know this can suggest that their children use water as the primary thirst quencher instead of soft drinks (Hannaford 1995).

Figure 3.3 summarizes this chapter's suggestions on what parents can do from birth to help their children be ready for school.

Practical Suggestions

It may seem as if there's little that educators can do about all of this. It's parents who get children ready to learn, after all. But this issue is so important that we must do *something*. We can't afford *not* to take action. There are three levels we can work at to influence some of these readiness areas: students, staff, and community.

Because we already influence them in many other ways, let's start with students. We can talk to them about nutrition and what stimulates better thinking, learning, and recall. We can ask them to do projects on nutrition to research the impact of various foods. We can ask them to keep a private journal so that they can begin to link up what they eat with how they feel and do in school. Guest speakers can provide some novelty or credibility on the subject. Maybe, most important, teachers and parents can role model good "eating-to-learn" nutrition.

At the staff level, we can influence what's served for school breakfasts or lunches. We can change what's put in the vending machines. We can provide information to the district office about

Figure 3.3

School Readiness: What Can Parents Do?

	0–18 Months	**18–60 Months**
Emotion	Provide loving care, safety, healthy stress response, hugs, laughter, smiles; bond with your child; avoid threats	Role model cause-and-effect feelings, empathy; provide a joyful home; set clear rules; avoid yelling
Motor	Encourage crawling, sitting, pointing; promote the use of balls, rattles, a variety of toys; provide mobiles; handle, touch, and rock your child frequently	Encourage games (like hide-and-seek), spinning, drawing, walking, running, balance activities; give your child freedom to explore (with safety); play and encourage the playing of instruments
Vision	Use many objects, a variety of movements, color identification; schedule eye exams; avoid TV	Play attention games and eye-hand coordination activities; teach how to focus; provide outdoor time; avoid TV; schedule eye exams
Auditory	Provide exposure to short phrases and high volume of coherent input; repeat sounds; use melodies; monitor for ear infections	Provide exposure to longer sentences, second languages, larger vocabulary, a variety of contexts; schedule regular ear exams
Thinking	Be overcurious about your child's world, do simple counting, demonstrate cause and effect	Use demonstrations, ask plenty of questions, teach basic math and principles of motion and volume
Music	Sing lullabies; give your child rattles; repeat rhymes; provide early exposure to common traditional songs and other nursery tunes	Sing; play instruments; listen to structured, harmonic music; provide exposure to more variety in kinds of music.
Nutrition	Mother's milk is still best; avoid excess juice; ensure sufficient nutrients; provision of moderate fats OK	Introduce a wide variety of foods; begin balanced meals high in fiber and vegetables; use vitamins

nutrition for learning. At the school open house, we can offer parents a talk and a handout on "Eating to Learn." We also can influence the district office if the school's start time needs to be changed. Many schools around the country have already successfully done this.

Finally, we ought to engage both school and community resources to educate parents on how to get their children ready for school. Many parents simply don't have access to information, or they think they already know it. Create alliances with local hospitals, the chamber of commerce, or local businesses to get the word out. Prepare flyers and provide free sessions for parents on the benefits of getting their children ready to learn. Talk to them about motor development, crawling, and how it affects reading and writing skills. Encourage them to talk more, play music, and solve more problems. Share with them the impact of television and some easy-to-use alternatives.

4 Enriched Environments and the Brain

Humans are born more helpless than any other mammal. That mixed blessing means that the infant can't take care of itself very well and that it can customize its growing brain for the world it encounters. This "neural customizing" can come from exposure to a barren wasteland of random stimuli or a rich landscape of thoughtful sensory input.

"It used to be that we thought the brain was hard-wired and that it didn't change . . . [but] positive environments can actually produce physical changes in the developing brain," says Frederick Goodwin, former director of the National Institute of Mental Health (in Kotulak 1996, p. 46). This chapter focuses on the importance of enrichment. We know enough to say the environment ought to be rich. But, practically, what are the specific components of an "enriched" environment?

Environmental Influence

The pendulum has swung over the last 100 years. For many decades, those who believed character and intelligence are mostly up to our genes ("nature") argued for their position and dominated national debates. They quoted studies about the "spelling gene," the "music gene," and even a "math gene." But in time, those convinced of the influence of the environment ("nurture") raised their voices long enough to garner public attention for their cause.

Today, consensus tells us that heredity provides about 30 to 60 percent of our brain's wiring, and 40 to 70 percent is the environmental impact. Why the variation? It depends on what specific trait or behavior you're considering. Male pattern baldness is on the X chromosome, which comes from the mother. If it is strongly expressed in your parents and grandparents, your chances of inheriting and expressing it are close to 100 percent. If you're a female and your mother was a strong leader, your likelihood of also being a strong leader may be closer to 30 percent. This lowered number reflects the complex environmental variables of circumstances, opportunity, and skills learned.

As educators, we can most influence the "nurture" aspect of students. While this chapter focuses on what enriches the brain, it also looks at the overall quality of the learning environment. Because of that, we must follow a cardinal rule when it comes to appreciating how the brain reacts to certain influences: Start by removing threats from the learning environment. No matter how excited you are about adding positives to the environment, first work to eliminate the negatives. Those include embarrassment, finger-pointing, unrealistic deadlines, forcing kids to stay after school, humiliation, sarcasm, a lack of resources, or simply being bullied. There is no evidence that threats are an effective way to meet long-term academic goals. Once threats are gone, we can go to work on the enrichment process.

Our Malleable Brain

In 1967, brain pioneer Marian Diamond, a University of California at Berkeley neuroanatomist, discovered an amazing malleability to the brain (Diamond 1967). Her studies—and subsequent research by dozens of colleagues—have changed the way we think about our brains. The brain can literally grow new connections with environmental stimulation. Diamond says, "When we enriched the environment, we got brains with a thicker cortex, more dendritic branching, more growth spines and larger cell bodies" (Healy 1990, p. 47). This means the brain cells communicate better with one another. There are more support cells, too. This can happen within 48 hours after the stimulation. Later studies support the conclusion that these are predictable and highly significant effects.

It's the *process* of making connections that counts. This suggests a possible cause for the enhanced learning capacity that many report—the increased neural stimulation. Smarter people probably do have a greater number of neural networks, and they're more intricately woven together. These changes match up favorably with those gained from complex experiences, specifically with learning and memory (Black et al. 1990). This view suggests that the environment affects the wiring of the brain as much as the person's actual experiences.

Dendritic branching was easy to find, but the evidence of synaptic plasticity is relatively recent. We now know how the brain modifies itself structurally; it's dependent on the type and amount of usage (Healy 1990; Green, Greenough, and Schlumpf 1983). Synaptic growth varies depending on which kind of activity is given. For novel motor learning, new synapses are generated in the cerebellar cortex. From exercise (repeated motor learning), the brain develops greater density of blood vessels in the molecular layer (Black et al. 1990). Some researchers found that an area of the midbrain involved in attentional processing—the superior colliculus—grew 5 to 6 percent more in an enriched environment (Fuchs, Montemayor, and Greenough 1990). Using fMRI (Functional Magnetic Resonance Imaging) technology, researchers at the University of Pennsylvania discovered that our brain has areas that are only stimulated by letters, not words or symbols (Lasley 1997). This suggests that new experiences (like reading) can get wired into the malleable brain. In other words, as you vary the type of environment, the brain varies the way it develops.

Yet all of this can get tricky. A student's early sensory deprivation can play a role. "If there is a bad experience, the wrong synapses are shed and the system malfunctions," says University of Illinois neuroscientist William Greenough (1997). Retaining excess synapses can be harmful, as in the case of Fragile X mental retardation. At school, there's more interest than ever in creating the right kind of enriching environments. That's for good reason. One of the most convincing arguments comes from the former director of the Institute of Mental Health, Frederick Goodwin. He says, "[T]here is now increasing understanding that the environment can affect you. . . [;] you can't make a 70 IQ person into a 150 IQ person, but you can change their IQ measure in different ways, perhaps as much as 20 points up or down, based on the environment" (Kotulak 1996). That's a 40-point range! Just how much can a school affect the brain? Neuroscientist Bob Jacobs confirms that animal research on brain enrichment translates directly to human brains. He

found that in autopsy studies on graduate students, they had up to 40 percent more connections than the brains of high school dropouts. The group of graduate students who were involved in challenging activities showed over 25 percent more overall "brain growth" than the control group. Yet education alone was not enough. Frequent new learning experiences and challenges were critical to brain growth. The brains of graduate students who were "coasting" through school had fewer connections than those who challenged themselves daily (Jacobs, Schall, and Scheibel 1993). Challenging sensory stimulation has been rightfully compared to a brain "nutrient." Figure 4.1 illustrates the differences between impoverished and enriched neurons.

FIGURE 4.1

How Enrichment Changes the Structure of Brain Cells

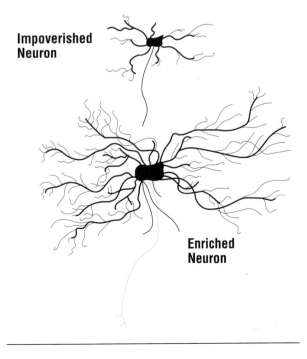

Impoverished Neuron

Enriched Neuron

Wayne State neurobiologist Harold Chugani points out that the school-age brain almost "glows" with energy consumption, burning at 225 percent of the adult levels of glucose. The brain learns fastest and easiest during the early school years. It nearly explodes with spectacular growth as it adapts with stunning precision to the world around it. During this time, stimulation, repetition, and novelty are essential to laying the foundations for later learning. The outside world is the growing brain's real food. It takes in the smells, sounds, sights, tastes, and touch and reassembles the input into countless neural connections. As the brain begins to make sense of the world, it creates a neural farmland.

Enrichment for Whom?

The myth for many years was that only certain "gifted and talented" students would most benefit from enrichment programs. Nothing could be further from the truth. The human brain is born with well over a trillion connections. Many new synapses are created with early sensory development, but any excess synapses are later shed. Greenough, a pioneer in enrichment studies, says that experience determines which synapses are shed or, more important, which are retained. This forms the "wiring diagram" upon which subsequent development builds (Begley 1996, p. 56). Our brain has a "baseline" of neural connectivity, and enrichment adds to it. Students can graduate from school with a "baseline" or an "enriched brain." Can we really afford to rob all of the "nongifted" students of their biological destiny to grow an enriched brain?

Rutgers neuroscientist Paula Tallal comments on this critical learning opportunity that everyone should get. "Don't wait. You don't get another window of opportunity like that," she says (in Kotulak 1996, p. 33). It's much easier, for example, to learn to play an instrument or learn a foreign language before age 10 than at any other time. But only the magnet school populations and gifted and talented students have received that kind of exposure. It's easy to understand why parents want to have their children labeled as "gifted." To miss that chance might doom their child to a "neural wasteland."

What Constitutes Enrichment?

Endless experiments have been done on both animals and humans to determine what conditions predictably and precisely build a better brain. William Greenough, who has studied the effects of enriching environments for over 20 years, says two things are particularly important in growing a better brain. The critical ingredients in any purposeful program to enrich the learner's brain are that first the learning is challenging, with new information or experiences. Often novelty will do it, but it must be challenging. Second, there must be some way to learn from the experience through interactive feedback.

Challenge is important; too much or too little and students will give up or get bored. Mental challenge can come about with new material, adding degree of difficulty, or through limiting the resources. This includes varying time, materials, access, expectations, or support in the learning process. Novelty is important, too. Change in the decor on the classroom walls every two to four weeks is valuable, but have the students do it for best enrichment. Change instructional strategies often: use computers, groups, field trips, guest speakers, pairings, games, student teaching, journaling, or multi-age projects (see fig. 4.2).

FIGURE 4.2

Maximizing Brain Growth

Challenge + *Feedback*

problem solving	**specific**
critical thinking	**multi-modal**
relevant projects	**timely**
complex activities	**learner controlled**

Second, maximize learner feedback. Because feedback reduces uncertainty, it increases coping abilities while lowering the pituitary-adrenal stress responses. Even in the absence of control, feedback has value (Hennessy, King, McClure, and Levine 1977). The brain itself is exquisitely designed to operate on feedback, both internal and external (Harth 1995). What is received at any one brain level depends on what else is happening at that level. And what is sent to the next level depends on the things already happening at that level. In other words, our whole brain is self-referencing. It decides what to do based on what has just been done. Without our magnificent system of feedback, we would be unable to learn. For example, after a student writes a paper in the classroom, the peer editing process is a superb way to get feedback.

Understandably, other learners can be the greatest asset in the learning environment. But many traditional environments are still not organized to take advantage of this opportunity. The best types of groups may be multi-age and multi-status groups (Caine and Caine 1994). While there may be little "hard biological research" on the value of cooperative groups, clearly they do two important things. When we feel valued and cared for, our brain releases the neurotransmitters of pleasure: endorphins and dopamine. This helps us enjoy our work more. Another positive is that groups provide a superb vehicle for social and academic feedback. When students talk to other students they get specific feedback on their ideas as well as their behaviors.

Several conditions make feedback more effective. The reaction must be specific, not general. A video game and a computer both give specific feedback, so does peer editing of a student's story. Group interaction provides feedback because it gives so much dramatic evidence, like nonverbals. Building a classroom model or playing a learning game gives interactive feedback. Feedback is ordinarily most useful for learners when it's immediate. Occasionally, a stressed or threatened learner will prefer delayed feedback. Greenough says the ideal feedback involves choice; it can be generated and modified at will. If it's hard to get at, or the performance cannot be altered once feedback is received, the brain doesn't learn quickly. Immediate and self-generating feedback can come from many sources: having posted criteria for performance, checking against personal goals, using a computer, or when the student checks with a parent or teacher from another grade level.

What should be the content of enrichment? Fortunately, the sources are endless. Here, we'll address just five of them: reading and language, motor stimulation, thinking and problem solving, the arts, and the surroundings.

Enrichment Through Reading and Language

Without exposure to new words, a youngster will never develop the cells in the auditory cortex to discriminate both between and among sounds well. Parents ought to read to their children beginning at 6 months, not wait until they're 4 or 5. Before puberty, most children will learn any language without a "foreigner's accent." The supply of cells and connection in the brain are ready and available to be used for it. There are enough for us to learn even the lightest nuances in pronunciation.

But after puberty, the connections have almost disappeared, and the potential cells for language have been usurped by other more aggressive cells for other functions. Schools ought to expose children to larger, more challenging vocabularies and to foreign languages by age 12. Neuronal loss and synaptic pruning make the acquisition of second languages more difficult with each passing year.

The more vocabulary the child hears from his or her teachers, the greater the lifelong vocabulary. An easy way to get the larger vocabulary is for teachers to role model it, expect it, and make it part of the learning. Reading is also a great way to develop vocabulary, though not by forcing it early on students. For some learners' brains, the "normal" time to learn to read is age 3 or 4. For others, the "normal" time is age 8. There can be, in fact, a spread in differences from a few months to 5 years in completely normal, developing brains. A 6-year-old who does not read might not be "developmentally delayed." In many countries, including Sweden, Denmark, Norway, and New Zealand (all with high literacy levels), formal reading instruction begins as late as age 7 or 8 (Hannaford 1995).

While reading is helpful for stimulating the growing brain, writing is another way to develop vocabulary. Usually we teach children printing before cursive. That makes little sense because the typical brain has not yet developed to make the fine visual-motor distinctions necessary. Children still have trouble with the lower case Ds and Bs as well as H, N, A, and E. The frustration children experience is for a reason: Their brains are not yet ready for it. Cursive is much easier, and it's better to teach that first. With the advance of technology and specifically computer keyboards, printing is less important today than 50 years ago.

The brains of children with language disorders are too balanced. That's not good, says language expert Paula Tallal. When both sides are equal, the left hemisphere is underpowered; the left side should be physically bigger and more active than the right hemisphere. A bigger, faster left brain means it can make fine distinctions in the sounds heard. This means words are distinct, not like a running stream of watery noise. That's what many dyslexics hear—words that run together. New software programs that stretch out the words until the brain can learn to sort them out are about 80 percent successful in retraining the brain, says Tallal (in Begley 1996, p. 62).

Enrichment Through Motor Stimulation

Is exercise or movement good for the brain? Keep in mind that repeating a movement or exercise is just doing what we already know how to do. Enrichment for brain stimulation is doing something new. Lyelle Palmer of Winona State University has been documenting the beneficial effects of early motor stimulation on learning for many years. He has used eye-hand coordination tasks, spinning, tumbling, rocking, pointing, counting, jumping, and ball toss activities to stimulate the early neural growth patterning. Palmer's "Chance to Learn Project" at the Shingle Creek Elementary School in Minneapolis showed positive effects on students through the Metropolitan Readiness Test, Test of Visual Perception, and the Otis Group Intelligence Test (Palmer 1980). In similar studies, the experimental group consistently outperformed the control group.

The benefits of early motor stimulation don't end in elementary school; there is tremendous value in novel motor stimulation throughout secondary school and the rest of our life (Brink 1995). Schools ought to make a planned program of specific motor stimulation mandatory in K-1 grades, but they also should integrate physical activity across the curriculum. In sports, we expect learners to use their brains for counting, planning, figuring, and problem solving. Every athlete is highly engaged in cognitive functions. It makes sense that we'd expect students to use their bodies for kinesthetic learning in the academic classes (see fig. 4.3).

Enrichment Through Thinking and Problem Solving

The single best way to grow a better brain is through challenging problem solving. This creates new dendritic connections that allow us to make even more connections. The brain is ready for simple, concrete problem solving at age 1 or 2. But the more complicated variety usually has to wait. There's a spurt of dendritic branching in the right hemisphere between 4 and 7 and in the left hemi-

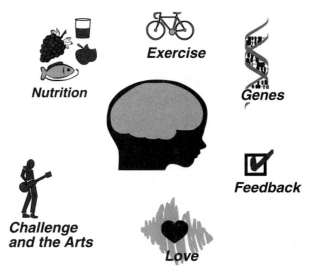

FIGURE 4.3

Key Factors That Influence Early Brain Development and Academic Achievement

Nutrition · **Exercise** · **Genes** · **Feedback** · **Love** · **Challenge and the Arts**

sphere between 9 and 12 (Hannaford 1995). Both sides are fully developed and usually ready for complex abstractions by ages 11 to 13. By then, the major bridge between left and right hemispheres, the corpus callosum, is fully matured. At that point it carries four billion messages per second across its 200–300 million nerve fibers and is ready for extra challenges. Some maturing of the brain continues into the mid-20s.

Kids need complex, challenging problems to solve. But problem solving is not limited to one area of the brain. After all, you can solve a problem on paper, with a model, with an analogy or metaphor, by discussion, with statistics, through artwork, or during a demonstration. As a result, there are as many neural pathways as we need to develop in children's brains as there are ways to solve a problem. That means it's critical to expose students to a variety of approaches to solving problems (Gardner 1993). When students feel more capable of solving a problem, their thoughts change their body's chemistry. Stanford University's Albert Bandura found that when the feelings of competence increased, the subjects in the test released fewer catacholomines, the body's natural chemical response to stress.

Surprisingly, it doesn't matter to the brain whether it ever comes up with an answer. The neural growth happens because of the process, not the solution. A student could go to school for 12 years, rarely get right answers, and still have a well-developed brain. Some learners simply choose harder and harder problems to solve. That may stimulate the release of noradrenaline and also create dendritic growth. Richard Haier of the Brain Imaging Center at the University of California at Irvine says, "The newer and more difficult the video game, the more neural activity" (in Marquis 1996, p. B-2). More intelligent people work their brains harder initially, then coast later on. Facing novel stimuli, higher IQ brains fire more neurons initially, bringing more resources to bear (Howard 1994). There's a much higher consumption of glucose while learning a new game versus when the game is mastered and the player is finally getting high scores. At the level of "mastery," the brain is coasting.

All of the typical puzzles, word games, hypothetical problems, and real-world problems are good for the brain. But be patient: The ability to succeed at one type of puzzle does not mean you'll be good at another. That's why someone is often good at crosswords but not jigsaw puzzles. Or they might be good at *Scrabble* and *Jeopardy*, but weak at cards and dominoes. The neural pathways that help us to excel at thinking skills are so specific that the whole concept of being "smart" or "gifted

and talented" has been called into question (Gardner 1983). It makes sense to encourage youngsters to do any problem-solving activity; the more real-life, the better. Also good are science experiments or building projects. Sadly, only 5 percent of all 11-year-olds have developed formal reasoning skills; that number is 25 percent by age 14. By adulthood, that percentage goes up to only 50 percent of the population (Epstein 1986).

Enrichment Through the Arts

For most of the twentieth century, a strong arts program meant you were raising a culturally aware child. But today's biology suggests that arts can help lay the foundation for later academic and career success. A strong art foundation builds creativity, concentration, problem solving, self-efficacy, coordination, and values attention and self-discipline.

The Musical Brain. We've all heard about the value of music as a component of enriched learning. Many schools offer music education in so-called gifted programs. But what evidence is there that daily music education ought to be universal, for every K-12 student? Is it merely anecdotal or has the new research on the brain caught up? In a nutshell, the evidence is persuasive that (1) our brain may be designed for music and arts and (2) a music and arts education has positive, measurable, and lasting academic and social benefits. In fact, considerable evidence suggests a broad-based music and arts education should be required for every student in the country.

Music is not a "right-brained frill." Robert Zatorre, neuropsychologist at the Montreal Neurological Institute, says, "I have very little doubt that when you're listening to a real piece of music, it is engaging the entire brain" (in Shreeve 1996,

p. 96). Reading music engages both sides of the brain, said the late Justine Sergent of the Montreal Neurological Institute. Once anyone learns how to read, compose, or play music, their left brain gets very involved. How does music fit with the concept of enrichment? Think of music as a tool for usage in at least three possible categories: for arousal, as a carrier of words, and as a primer for the brain. Arousal means the music either increases or decreases the attentional neurotransmitters. An example of "perk up" music could be the theme from "Rocky." Relaxing music might include a waterfall or soft piano melodies. This type of music can significantly affect the states of the learners. And that, of course, can affect the learning. A study of 8th and 9th graders reported in *Principal* magazine showed that students' reading comprehension substantially improved with background music (Giles 1991).

A second use of music is as a carrier. In this case, the melody of the music acts as the vehicle for the words themselves. You may have noticed how easily students pick up the words to new songs. It's the melody that helps them learn the words. How did you learn the alphabet? Most likely it was through the alphabet song. You heard that song over and over as an infant. When it was time to learn the letters, you simply "glued" the letters to the notes of the melody. The result was a quickly learned alphabet.

There is a third, and quite powerful, use of music. It can actually prime the brain's neural pathways. Neurons are constantly firing. What distinguishes the "neural chatter" from clear thinking is the speed, sequence, and strength of the connections. These variables constitute a pattern of firing that can be triggered or "primed" by certain pieces of music. As an example, have you ever put on a

piece of music to help you get a task done like cleaning the house or garage?

To review the evidence, we turn to Norman Weinberger, a neuroscientist at the University of California at Irvine. He's an expert on the auditory cortex and its response to music. He says, "An increasing amount of research findings supports the theory that the brain is specialized for the building blocks of music" (Weinberger 1995, p. 6). Much research suggests that the auditory cortex responds to pitch and tones rather than simply raw sound frequencies, and individual brain cells process melodic contour. Music may, in fact, be critical for later cognitive activities.

Lamb and Gregory (1993) found a high correlation between pitch discrimination and reading skills. Mohanty and Hejmadi (1992) found that musical dance training boosted scores on the Torrance Test of Creativity. What causes the correlation? It's all in the rate and pattern that brain cells fire. Frances Rauscher says, "We know the neural firing patterns are basically the same for music appreciation and abstract reasoning. . . ." (in Mandelblatt 1993, p. 13). In the well-publicized "Mozart Effect" study at the University of California at Irvine, there were three listening conditions. One was relaxation music. The other, the control, had no music. The third had Mozart's "Sonata for Two Pianos in D Major." After just 10 minutes of headset listening, Rauscher, Shaw, Levine, Ky, and Wright (1993) found that the Mozart selection temporarily improved spatial temporal reasoning. Rauscher notes that it's a causal relationship, not a correlation. This study was the first ever to show listening to music as the cause of improved spatial intelligence. Other studies had merely shown that music was a contributing factor or had indirect correlations. Listening to Mozart before testing is valuable; listening during a test would cause neural competition by interfering with the neural firing pattern.

A survey of studies suggest that music plays a significant role in enhancing a wide range of academic and social skills. For one, it activates procedural (body) memory and therefore, is learning that lasts (Dowling 1993). In addition, James Hanshumacher (1980) reviewed 36 studies, of which 5 were published and the remaining were unpublished dissertations. He concluded that arts education facilitates language development, enhances creativity, boosts reading readiness, helps social development, assists general intellectual achievement, and fosters positive attitudes toward school (Hanshumacher 1980). After all, music is a language that can enhance the abilities of children who don't excel in the expression of verbal thinking.

Does evidence support the value of singing? Music researcher M. Kalmar found that music has many positive school correlates. Between the two groups, only the experimental group had better abstract conceptual thinking, stronger motor development, coordination, creativity, and verbal abilities. Another study (Hurwitz, Wolff, Bortnick, and Kokas 1975) concluded that the music groups (trained only in folk songs) "exhibited significantly higher reading scores than did the control group, scoring in the 88th percentile versus the 72nd percentile." Singing is good stimulation for the brain, "a means to promote both musical competence and full development. . ." (Weinberger 1996).

Art Enrichment. How does art research hold up? Art education has gotten a tremendous boost from discoveries in neuroscience. The old paradigm was that left-brain thinking was the home of the necessary "higher-order" thinking skills, and right-brain activities were frills. That paradigm is dead wrong. Current research tells us that much learning is "both-brained." Musicians usually process melodies in their left hemispheres. PET scans of problem solvers show activations in not just the left frontal lobes but other areas used to store music, art, and movement (Kearney 1996). Many of our greatest scientific thinkers, like Einstein, have talked about the integration of imagination into scientific pursuit.

There has been worldwide success of the neuropsychological art therapy model, or NAT (Parente and Anderson-Parente 1991, McGraw 1989). The use of art not just to draw but to teach thinking and build emotive expressiveness and memory has been a remarkable demonstration of the brain's plasticity. By learning and practicing art, the human brain actually rewires itself to make more and stronger connections. Researchers learned this by using it as therapy for the brain damaged (Kolb and Whishaw 1990). Jean Houston says that arts stimulate body awareness, creativity, and sense of self. In fact, she says, "The child without access to arts is being systematically cut off from most of the ways in which he can experience the world" (in Williams 1977).

Policymakers and educators are often looking for data to support the role of arts. In Columbus, Ohio, the results were quite measurable. Talk to principal James Gardell at Douglas Elementary. This predominately arts-centered school has achievement scores 20 points above the district norms in 5 of 6 academic areas. Demand for their program is strong; more than 100 children are on the school's "wait list." Does the art emphasis make a difference? "There's a definite link," says Gardell (1997). Other schools in the area like Duxbury,

Clinton, and Fair Avenue are experiencing similar academic success through an arts emphasis.

Norman Weinberger states emphatically that the argument that art and music are frills "finds no objective support." He summarizes, "Teachers should be encouraged to bring or increase music in the classroom" (Weinberger 1996). But do they need to be experts or music teachers? Music specialists are preferred, but in the absence of an expert, something is better than nothing.

Enrichment Through the Surroundings

Teachers often like to share their "enriched classroom" with others. They proudly show off all of the affirmations, mobiles, posters, colors, and pictures on the walls as symbols of enrichment. Do visuals on the wall help stimulate learning? Remember that enrichment comes from challenge and feedback, not artistic merit or aesthetic enjoyment. Here, the word enrichment is obviously being used very loosely.

Does this mean that we should encourage bare-walled classrooms? Absolutely not! While the busy, decorative classrooms probably have debatable enrichment value, they do serve other very valuable purposes. They can be a source of inspiration, affirmation, and content. They can help learners feel safe, comfortable, or keep up with the learning (Debes 1974). Do you think it matters what we look at? In hospitals, a controlled study found that patients with "a view room" recovered faster than those who stared at a brick wall. The stimulation apparently affects more than well-being; it also feeds the brain (Urich 1984). A rich classroom environment full of posters, mobiles, maps, pictures, and graphic organizers will be taken in at some level by most students.

Practical Suggestions

We've come to understand the two critical ingredients in enrichment are challenge and feedback. Since what's challenging for one student may not be challenging for another, this makes a tremendous argument for choice in the learning process, including self-paced learning, and more variety in the strategies used to engage learners better. Examples of choice include the student's option to select the complexity or type of a project. In addition, choice may include student decisions about computers, videos, partners, seating, and the final format of the expected end result. Variety means that regardless of what students choose, it's the educator's imperative to expose them to a wide variety of methodology. This means rotating individual and group work, drama, music, presentations, self-directed work, computers, guest speakers, and travel to new locations, even if it's just to another classroom in the school.

To increase enrichment, it's time to reaffirm the integration of the arts and movement into the curriculum. The national Goals 2000 statement had little mention of the arts; that makes poor sense in lieu of their long-term value. The arts and movement are often excellent forms of challenge and feedback. Norman Weinberger calls for "widespread educational trials" in arts and music education. In the same way that a new drug is tested with controlled studies under the eye of the FDA, schools ought to conduct systematic and formally documented trials with art and movement education.

To do that, we might

• Form better alliances among schools and local universities in order to get better studies initiated and tracked.

- Increase the appropriate use of music, including singing, listening to music, and playing instruments.

- Increase the richness and variety of student options in the environment through, for example, seating, lighting, and peripherals.

Two rules come from the field of brain research and enrichment. One is to eliminate threat, and the other is to enrich like crazy. Before we understood the collective impact of an enriched environment, it may have been acceptable to justify a minimalist classroom. Gone are the days in which any teacher could justify a barren classroom with one-way lecture as the only input. Today, the evidence is overwhelming that enriched environments do grow a better brain. In addition, the early developing brain grows fastest and is the most ready for change. That opportunity must be seized.

While the case for enrichment is strong, what happens if we don't enrich? In "teenage" rats, a boring environment had a more powerful *thinning* effect on the cortex than did a positive, enriched environment on *thickening* the cortex (Diamond 1998, p. 31). Boredom is more than annoying for teens—it may be thinning their brains! Fortunately, studies show the shrinkage can be reversed in as little as four days (p. 31).

Considering that schools provide a forum for an average of 6 hours a day, 180 days a year, for 13 years, that's a potential exposure of over 14,000 hours. Thus, educators have a significant moral and ethical responsibility for enhancing or limiting the lifetime potential of a human being. Will those hours be spent nurturing a better brain or literally narrowing the boundaries of that potential? The answer is easy. Let's all enrich like crazy.

Getting the Brain's Attention

Getting students' attention and keeping it has been the brass ring in the world of teaching. Many among us admire Hollywood teachers from movies like *Stand and Deliver, Dead Poets Society,* and *Dangerous Minds.* They rivet students'—and our own—attention, and we respect colleagues who can imitate their methods in real life.

But what if such a teaching model were wrong?

What if getting attention ought to be the exception—not the rule? What if we're placing inappropriate and often unreasonable demands on students, and the more that a teacher has a student's attention, the less genuine learning can happen? That's the focus of this chapter: attention and its relationship to learning in light of recent brain research.

The Attentive Brain

As each new school year begins, well-meaning teachers quickly classify students into two categories: those who pay attention and those who don't. Translated, that means the "good kids" and the "problem kids." Consequently, an enormous amount of energy is invested in getting kids "to be good." The stakes are high, and the tools include promises, rewards, noisemakers, threats, raised voices, and gimmicks. Nearly every experienced teacher has surefire ways to get attention. For years, new teachers eagerly modeled these "top-gun" teacher methods. They, too, wanted to get student attention and keep it. But is that really good teaching?

For much of the 20th century, attention was the domain of psychology. But in the last decade, several strands of research have mounted a powerful case about the role biological factors play in attention and learning. We now know the purpose of attention seems to be (1) to promote survival and (2) to extend pleasurable states. For example, research has revealed:

• Attentional systems are located throughout the brain.

• The contrasts of movement, sounds, and emotions (like threat) consume most of our attention.

• Chemicals play the most significant role in attention.

• Genes also may be involved in attention.

When we are awake, we have an important decision to make every single moment: where to turn our attention. A normal person makes this decision about 100,000 times a day. The brain is always paying attention to something; its survival depends on it. In general, when we talk about "paying attention" in an educational context, we are referring to external, focused attention. That means the student is looking at the teacher and thinking only of the material presented.

However, the brain's attentional systems have countless other possibilities. Attention can be external or internal, focused or diffused, relaxed or vigilant. We ask students to be able to identify appropriate objects of attention (often it's a teacher); to sustain that attention until instructed otherwise (even if it's a lecture that lasts for an hour); and to ignore other, often more interesting, stimuli in the environment. This request is entirely reasonable when the learning is relevant, engaging, and chosen by the learner. When those conditions are not met, classroom attention is a statistical improbability.

We now know that the two primary determinates of our attention are the sensory input (such as a threat or an appealing opportunity) and the brain's chemical "flavor of the moment." One is focused like a laser beam, the other is scattered, more like a set of Christmas tree lights. Both are constantly regulating our attention, so let's explore each of them.

The Pathways of Attention

The attention process consists of alarm, orientation, identification, and decision. This sequential, laser beam process is akin to, "Whoops, something's happening," then, "Where?" and finally "What is it?" The answer to the final question will usually tell us how long we ought to attend to it. Attention is expressed in a student when there's greater flow of information in the specific target area of the brain's pathways relative to the surrounding pathways. In short, when specialized brain activity is up, attention is up. Figure 5.1 illustrates the various areas of the brain involved in getting and keeping attention.

How does your brain know what specifically to pay attention to in the moment? The secret is that our visual system (which sends more than 80 per-

FIGURE 5.1

Areas Involved in Getting and Keeping Your Attention

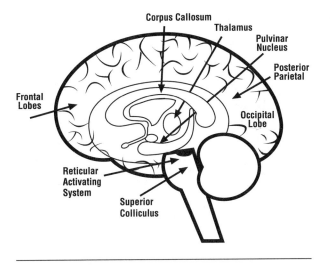

cent of information to the brain in nonimpaired learners) is not a one-way street. Information flows both ways, back and forth from our eyes, to the thalamus, to the visual cortex. This feedback is the mechanism that "shapes" our attention so that we can focus on one particular thing, like a teacher lecturing or reading a book (Kosslyn 1992). Amazingly, the number of inputs that our "attention headquarters" gets as feedback *from* the cortex is nearly six times as high as the original input from the retina. That volume of feedback triggers certain selective neurons along the visual pathways to fire less often because their membranes are hyperpolarized to prevent normal processing. The proper attentional functioning means not just stimulating many new neurons but also suppressing unimportant information. Somehow, the brain corrects incoming images to help you stay attentive. What we see and attend to is a two-way balancing act of construction and feedback-maintenance of stimuli. When you are ignoring something, the brain has an innate mechanism for shutting down inputs.

The brain's susceptibility to paying attention is very much influenced by priming. We are more likely to see something if we are told to look for it or prompted on its location. Neuroimaging methods have shown increased neuronal firing in the frontal lobes and anterior cingulate when someone is working hard to pay attention. In general, the right parietal lobe is involved in attentional shifts. If you are looking for a teaching book you left in the classroom, your left frontal lobe tells the midbrain area how to sort incoming data. There, the lateral geniculate nucleus (LGN) suppresses the input of all other books, folders, pamphlets, boxes, and other book-sized objects that look anything like that book but are not the one you want (LaBerge 1995). Not only that, the mere thought of that book will trigger any similar book to your attention. By trying countless possibilities within seconds, the brain usually comes up with the goal: the book is found, it is declared lost, you lose interest, or you decide to continue searching.

Selective attention depends on suppression of irrelevant data and the amplification of relevant data. To a great deal, students succeed academically when they have the ability to "tune in" like a radio to an exact, focused "bandwidth." What's outside the bandwidth must be important to get your attention. If you want attention, provide a strong contrast from what you were just doing. We get used to a new smell within seconds, so it takes a new one to again get our attention. Teachers who raise their voices in an already too-noisy classroom may get frustrated. It makes more sense to use a highly contrasting signal system like a desktop bell, a raised hand, a playground whistle, or a dramatic change of location.

The Chemistry of Attention

Our brain's chemicals are the real life-blood of the attentional system and have a great deal to do with what students pay attention to at school. The chemicals include neurotransmitters, hormones, and peptides. Acetylcholine is a neurotransmitter that seems to be linked with drowsiness. In general, its levels are higher in the later afternoon and nighttime. Clearly, we are more alert with higher adrenaline levels. Researchers suspect that of all the chemicals, norepinephrine is the most involved in attention (Hobson 1994). Studies indicate that when we are drowsy or "out of it," our norepinephrine levels are usually low; when we are too "hyper" and stressed, the levels are too high.

Under stress and threat, the dominant chemicals in the brain include cortisol, vasopressin, and endorphins. The first two are particularly critical to our stress and threat responses. If a student is about to be called to the principal's office, the body's stress and threat response kicks in. Pulse is up, skin is flushed, and the body's "on edge." A change in chemicals means a likely change in behaviors. For example, if you want creativity from students, you may have found it works to get them out of a stressed state with a walk, music, humor, or storytelling.

Roller-Coaster Attention Cycles

You may have noticed that you have natural attentional highs and lows throughout the day. These are ultradian rhythms, one of our brain's key cycles lasting about 90–110 minutes. That means we have about 16 cycles lasting 24-hour period. The odd thing is that while we are used to "light and deep" sleep, we rarely connect this with typical high and low arousal-rest cycles during the day. Some students who are consistently drowsy in your class may be at the bottom of the their attentional cycle. Movements such as stretching or marching can help focus attention. Students should be encouraged to stand and stretch, without attracting attention, if they feel drowsy.

The brain shifts its cognitive abilities on those high and low cycles. There's literally a change in blood flow and breathing on these cycles that affects learning (Klein, Pilon, Prosser, and Shannahoff-Khalsa 1986). Our brain becomes alternately more efficient in processing either verbal or spatial information. These periods of alternating efficiency seem to correlate with a known rhythm, "the basic rest-activity cycle" (BRAC), discovered sometime ago via sleep research. In studies by Raymond Klein and Roseanne Armitage, eight subjects were tested for 3-minute periods every 15 minutes over an eight-hour day on two tasks, one predominantly verbal, the other spatial. The differences are significant; the upswing on verbal tasks went from an average score of 165 to 215 correct answers and a simultaneous downswing from 125 to 108 on spatial (Klein and Armitage 1979). This oscillation suggests that we will get lower scores if we test students at the wrong time. It makes a case for choice in the learning process and choice in the assessment process. Portfolios, which are compiled over time, are more inclusive and accurate than a "snapshot" test, since they may average in the highs and lows better. Figure 5.2 represents the brain's cycles through the day and night. Figure 5.3 represents electrical activity during brain wave states.

FIGURE 5.2

The Brain's 90–110 Minute High-Low Cycles

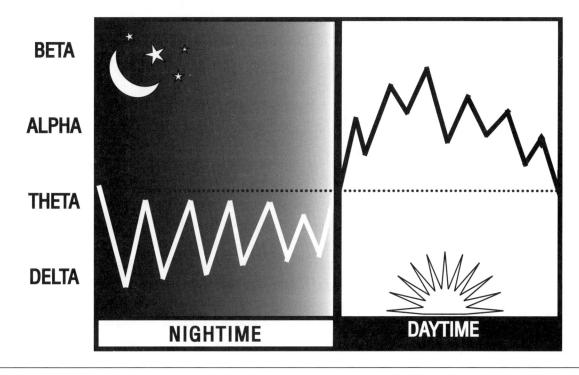

The daily low or "down" parts of the 90–110 minute cycle reflect the message from our brains: Take it easy. Several researchers say that mental breaks of up to 20 minutes several times a day increase productivity (Rossi and Nimmons 1991). Instead of fighting the lack of energy or alertness, educators can take advantage of it. Pearce Howard (1994) says that in general, workers need 5- to 10-minute breaks every hour and a half. Why would students or staff be any different? That would fit right into the "bottom" of the 90–110 minute cycle. In secondary schools, running from one classroom to another is not true "down time" for most students. These cycles make a good case for the use of block scheduling at the secondary level. With a longer block of time, the teacher can include break activities without feeling pressured to teach content every minute.

The Role of Inattention or "Processing Time"

Generally, the brain does poorly at continuous, high-level attention. In fact, genuine "external" attention can be sustained at a high and constant level for only a short time, generally 10 minutes or less. This leads us to the biological question, "What smart adaptive benefits might there be to having a shorter attention span?" Researchers suggest that there may be several good reasons. You are able to react quickly to predators and prey. It allows you to update your priorities by rechoosing

FIGURE 5.3

Brain Wave States Are Measures of Electrical Activity (cps = cycles per second)

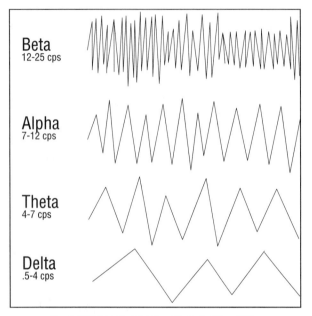

Beta
12-25 cps

Alpha
7-12 cps

Theta
4-7 cps

Delta
.5-4 cps

Key to Understanding the Specific Brain Wave States

Beta... High activity: debate, exercise, complex projects, competition
Alpha... Relaxed alertness: reading, writing, watching, problem solving
Theta... Deep susceptibility: drowsy, meditative, processing time
Delta... Nonconscious: deepest sleep, "dead to the world"

the object of your attention (LaBerge 1995). This affirms the value of focused learning time followed by diffused activities like reflection.

In the classroom, there are three reasons why constant attention is counterproductive. First, much of what we learn cannot be processed consciously; it happens too fast. We need time to process it. Second, in order to create new meaning, we need internal time. Meaning is always generated from within, not externally. Third, after each new learning experience, we need time for the learning to "imprint."

In fact, new physical skills can take up to six hours to solidify. Henry Holcomb of Johns Hopkins University asserts that other new learning contaminates the memory process. "We've shown that time itself is a very powerful component of learning," he adds (in Manning 1997). Our visual capacity, measured by bits per second and carried by the optical nerve, is in the tens of millions (Koch 1997). That's far too much to process consciously (Dudai 1997). In order to either proceed or figure it all out, a student must "go internal" and give up that "external" attention. We can't process it all consciously, so the brain continues to process information before and long after we are aware that we are doing it. As a result, many of our best ideas seem to pop out of the blue. As educators, we must allow for this creative time if we want new learning to occur. After completely new learning takes place, teachers should consider short, divergent activities like a ball toss or a walk that builds communication skills.

Humans are natural meaning-seeking organisms. But while the search is innate, the end result is not automatic. Because meaning is generated internally, external input conflicts with the possibility that learners can turn what they have just learned into something meaningful. You can either have your learners' attention or they can be making meaning, but never both at the same time. Therefore, teachers might allow students to have a small group discussion after new material is introduced to sort it out, generate questions, and propose what-if scenarios. Synapses strengthen when they are given time for neural connections to solidify because they don't need to respond to other competing stimuli. Cellular resources can be preserved and focused on critical synaptic junctions (see fig. 5.4).

Alcino Silva at Cold Spring Harbor Laboratory discovered that mice improved their learning with short training sessions punctuated by rest intervals

FIGURE 5.4

Allow Time for the Brain's Connections to Solidify

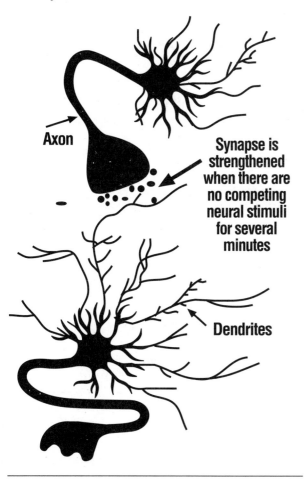

Axon

Synapse is strengthened when there are no competing neural stimuli for several minutes

Dendrites

(Lasley 1997). He says the rest time allows the brain to recycle CREB, an acronym for a protein switch crucial to long-term memory formation. Other research also suggests that periods of purposeful processing time, as an "incubation for learning," may be ideal (Scroth et al. 1993). It may be the down time, which we now know is not really "down," that's most important for new information processing. Learning can become more functional when external stimuli is shut down and the brain can link it to other associations, uses, and procedures. "This association and consolidation process can only occur during down time," says Alan Hobson of Harvard University. This finding suggests that we may want to allow for several minutes of reflection time after new learning. Writing in journals or discussing the new learning in small groups makes good sense for the learning brain.

The essential point here is that teachers must encourage "personal processing time" after new learning for material to solidify. The variety of options above reflect different student needs, learning styles, and intelligences. Cramming more content per minute, or moving from one piece of learning to the next, virtually guarantees that little will be learned or retained. In fact, many teachers who complain of having to do so much "reteaching" are the same ones trying to cram too much. How much processing time depends on the difficulty of the material and background of the learner. Teaching "heavy, new" content to novice learners may require processing time of 2–5 minutes every 10–15 minutes. But a review of old-hat material to well-rehearsed learners may require only a minute or so every 20 minutes. (See fig. 5.5.)

This old notion of continuous attention also is a problem for teachers themselves. Teachers need more personal and better quality down time during the day. With schedules that rarely allow for more than a moment of solitude or quiet, stress is the order of the day. The work schedule wreaks havoc on the teacher's high- and low-brain cycles. To stay alert, teachers often become caffeine junkies, consuming a steady stream of coffee and soft drinks. It makes sense for teachers to find a few moments for quiet time, if possible. If not, they should reduce their intake of carbohydrates that induce drowsiness and stay as physically

FIGURE 5.5

Factors That Influence Attention for Learning

Increase intrinsic motivation **Hook attention for 10–90 minutes**	**Increase apathy and resentment** **Hook attention for 10 minutes or less**
Choices **vs.**	*Required*
Provide choices: content, timing, work partners, projects, process, environment, or resources.	Directed 100%, no student input, resources restricted—for example, working alone
Relevant **vs.**	*Irrelevant*
Make it personal: relate to family, neighborhood, city, life stages, love, health, and so on	Impersonal, useless, out of context, and done only to pass a test
Engaging **vs.**	*Passive*
Make it emotional, energetic; make it physical; use learner-imposed deadlines and peer pressure	Disconnected from the real world, low interaction, lecture, seatwork, or video

active as possible with movement, stretching, and deep breathing.

Edison was famous for taking short, quick naps during the day. Some sleep experts now encourage employees to take a daily catnap. The Nike offices in Beaverton, Oregon, have a "relaxation room" for it. Even the FAA, which has banned pilot "catnaps," is considering a plan to allow power napping. Cornell University sleep researcher James Maas prescribes a 20-minute afternoon nap to combat fatigue. He says power nappers think more clearly and perform far better than their overtired colleagues. (Wallis 1996). For

today's K-2 teacher, it's fairly acceptable to have down time or nap time. For students age 8 and older, a 15-minute quiet "choice time" might allow for a nap, reading, reflection, writing, or drawing. The critical ingredient to down time or personal processing time is choice. If a teacher uses this time to assign seatwork or deadline-centered projects, it is *not* rest for the brain.

How Attention Affects Discipline

A classroom that is plagued by discipline problems may have many overlapping causes. One of the first places to start is with attention. Cut the length of focused attention time expected or required. Remember that the human brain is poor at non-stop attention. As a guideline, use 5–7 minutes of direct instruction for K–2, 8–12 minutes for grades 3–7, and 12–15 minutes for grades 8–12. After learning, the brain needs time for processing and rest. In a typical classroom, this means rotating mini-lectures, group work, reflection, individual work, and team project time.

The causes of quick-tempered, short-attention span behaviors are currently being explored by neuroscientists. Dopamine is a neurotransmitter known to regulate emotion, movement, and thought. Researchers have discovered that there's a genetic link between quick-tempered, novelty-seeking, and inattentive behaviors and a specific receptor gene for dopamine. Those students who have a longer DNA sequence in this gene score much higher on tests that measure novelty seeking and impulsiveness. The implications for this are significant: Some students will be out of control, but the cause of their behavior may be genes, not poor parenting (Hittman 1996). Teachers should set aside the label of misbehavior and simply deal with the behavior. Sometimes adding more active learning strategies is all it takes.

Attention Deficit

We've learned the brain is poorly designed for continuous, focused attention. The opposite, too much attention, is a form of attention deficit, too. Trying to pay attention to everything is as much a problem as not paying enough attention when appropriate. In the United States, attention deficit disorder (ADD) accounts for almost half of all child psychiatric referrals (Wilder 1996). Studies indicate that 1 of 20 children aged 6 to 10 and about 3 percent of all children under 19 are on ADD medications like Ritalin or Cylert. Prescriptions are currently at 1.5 million and climbing dramatically (Elias 1996). Some schools have as many as 10 percent on Ritalin.

ADD is not without controversy. While some researchers believe it is a specific medical disorder, others believe that the label masks many other more narrowly defined problems like poor hearing, bad eyesight, or inadequate nutrition. The current research on the biological underpinnings of ADD associates the disorder with several factors. A large sample of 102 children diagnosed with ADD found evidence of smaller attentional structures in the outermost right frontal lobe areas and basal ganglia (Wilder 1996). Those two areas are thought to be essential for directing focus and blocking out distractions. Second, there's evidence of faulty regulation of glucose metabolization and of the neurotransmitter norepinephrine. Finally, S. Milberger, Joseph Biederman, and their colleagues at Massachusetts General Hospital have discovered a striking connection between ADD and maternal smoking (George 1996).

Research suggests that other psychiatric disorders frequently occur with ADD making detection confusing. These include inability to form close relationships, anxiety, and stress trauma. Those who do have ADD are often fidgety, with scattered attention. The critical qualifying symptoms for a child to be diagnosed with ADD are that the symptoms must be both excessive and long term. The ability to focus attention and restrain inappropriate motor acts demonstrates not that children with ADD can't pay attention; they are paying attention to everything. They continually disengage from one signal in favor of the next irrelevant signal. Their system is low on norepinephrine, so the drug intervention (when appropriate) is to give it a stimulant.

Ritalin is a central nervous stimulant that inhibits the reuptake of dopamine and norepinephrine. ADD medications are usually amphetamines, which boost the "signal" of the more important information and help inhibit some of the distracting motor movements. Some students will outgrow the behavior; others won't. Researchers are uncertain what percentage of children with ADD are likely to continue into adulthood with the disorder. Hill and Schoener's model predicts a 50 percent decline every 5 years beyond childhood (George 1996).

Most psychiatrists today specify ADD symptoms as "predominantly inattentive," "predominantly hyperactive," or "combined." The most common characteristic, according to researchers, is "comorbidity." That's the phenomenon of finding more than one psychiatric disorder at a time. Frequently, the disorder co-occurs with conduct, anxiety, and learning disorders (Biederman et al. 1996). While most of the medical community has ruled out poor parenting, bad environments, or lack of nutrition, others feel differently. One of the most vocal, Thomas Armstrong, is the author of *The Myth of ADD*. He suggests many other variables are suspect, including a mismatch of teaching and learning styles, poor nutrition, and poor parenting (Armstrong 1995).

Many researchers believe that ADD is overdiagnosed. Too often kids are prescribed Ritalin after one short visit with their GP and no input from parents or teachers. But one might be equally distressed over the few kids who do have ADD and don't get help. For them, life is a horror movie they can't escape.

Detection and diagnosis of ADD is difficult. First, many students are misdiagnosed as ADD when their problem may be crowded classrooms, discipline difficulties, a teacher who demands an inappropriate amount of classroom attention, or a lack of self-discipline skills. Many times diet or allergies are contributing factors. The best solutions may be to make sure that the intervention assessing team and the student have first exhausted nonprescriptive options including changing classes or teachers. When medications are used, they should be monitored carefully to ensure results are in line with expectations.

Practical Suggestions

The old notion about attention was get it and keep it. Today, you can have students' attention 20–40 percent of the time and get terrific results. We know how to get attention: use contrast. In fact, nearly everything that is novel will garner attention; the contrast alone is enough. As classroom teachers well know, a student who cracks a joke, an uninvited visitor, threats, shocks, or bodily sounds will all get our attention. But that's not the kind of attention we have in mind.

A change in location is one of the easiest ways to get attention, because our brain's posterior attention system is specialized to respond to location rather than other cues like color, hue, shape, or motion (Ackerman 1992). For example, teachers can move to the back or side of the room during instruction. Students can move to the back of the room, the side, or even go outside for a moment. If it's appropriate, switch classrooms with another teacher for just one class or a day. Field trips are the greatest change of location and well worth it when organized well.

Overall, you'll want to provide a rich balance of novelty and ritual. Novelty ensures attentional bias, and ritual ensures that there are predictable structures for low stress. For novelty, use a surprising piece of music one day, ask students to bring in something that makes music the next. Have students present their learning to one another, then in small groups. Bring in a guest speaker from your own school. Use fun, energizing rituals for class openings, closings, and most of the repetitious classroom procedures and activities. A double clap and foot stomp may introduce an important daily summary. A change in voice tonality, tempo, volume, or accent gets attention. Props, noisemakers, bells, whistles, costumes, music, or singing can get attention. You can also include attention-getting rituals like raising a hand or a daily group clap. Then, intersperse the novelty to ensure the higher attentional bias.

These suggestions are for use once or twice a day, of course. Teachers need not become circus performers. To the contrary, in the best classrooms, the students are the "show." But teachers must recognize that constant changes in tempo and time for reflection are critical in learning. Once you have attention, make the most of it; otherwise you'll have to start over again.

6 How Threats and Stress Affect Learning

A part of the Hippocratic Oath says that the first rule in medicine is to do patients no harm. That may well apply to educators, too. Excess stress and threat in the school environment may be the single greatest contributor to impaired academic learning. That's a strong statement, but when you understand the many potential threats for students and how the brain reacts to each, it makes sense. This chapter focuses on the negative impact of threats and high stress on the brain, behavior, and learning.

Why Common Threats Fail

Threats have long served as the weapon of choice to regulate human behavior. When schools were optional, threats were less relevant; a student who was upset might have simply left. But today, students find that they must endure threats because their presence at school is mandated by law.

Teachers' most common threats to students include detention, lowered grades, or loss of school privileges. Detention has clout only if one of two variables is present: either the student could better use the time or staying after is a miserable experience. Many students don't have a better use of their time than staying after class. And if staying after is a miserable experience, the bad feelings "contaminate" the student's overall opinions about the teacher, classroom, and school. That damage can be deadly to long-term motivation and morale, so generally it's not worth it to detain students. Many students don't respond to lowered grades or a loss of privileges, so those threats can be tenuous. In short, on a purely behavioral level, threats make little sense. But what is happening on a more biological level?

Stress and Learning

When we feel stressed, our adrenal glands release a peptide called cortisol. Our body responds with cortisol whether it faces physical, environmental, academic, or emotional danger. This triggers a string of physical reactions including depression of the immune system, tensing of the large muscles, blood-clotting, and increasing blood pressure. It's the perfect response to the unexpected presence of a saber-toothed tiger. But in school, that kind of response leads to problems. Chronically high cortisol levels lead to the death of brain cells in the hippocampus, which is critical to explicit memory formation (Vincent 1990).

These physical changes are significant. Stanford scientist Robert Sapolsky found that atrophy levels in the hippocampus of Vietnam veterans with PTSD (post-traumatic stress disorder) ranged from 8 to 24 percent above the control group. Chronic stress also impairs a student's ability to sort out what's important and what's not (Gazzaniga 1988). Jacobs and Nadel (1985) suggest that thinking and memory are affected under stress; the brain's short-term memory and ability to form long-term memories are inhibited.

There are other problems. Chronic stress makes students more susceptible to illness. In one study, students showed a depressed immune system at test time; they had lower levels of an important antibody for fighting infection (Jermott and Magloire 1985). This may explain a vicious academic cycle: More test stress means more sickness, which means poor health and missed classes, which contribute to lower test scores. Figure 6.1 illustrates the differences between a stressed and an unstressed neuron. The stressed one has fewer and shorter dendrites. This deficiency impairs communications with other dendrites. What caused this dramatic difference?

FIGURE 6.1

How Social Stress Can Affect Neurons

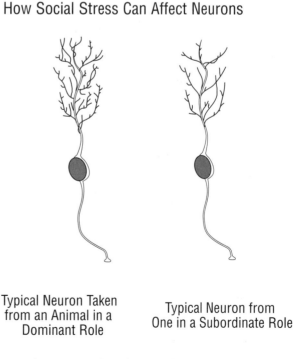

Typical Neuron Taken from an Animal in a Dominant Role

Typical Neuron from One in a Subordinate Role

Social position changes both attitude and behaviors. Part of the body and brain's reaction to these changes are elevated serotonin levels and changes in neural structure. This evidence suggests the value of varying the leadership in class groups.

A stressful physical environment is linked to student failure. Crowded conditions, poor student relationships, and even lighting can matter. Optometrist Ray Gottlieb says that school stress causes vision problems. That in turn impairs academic achievement and self-esteem. He says that, typically, a stressed child will constrict breathing and change how he or she focuses to adapt to the stress. This pattern hurts learning in the short and long run. Under stress, the eyes become more attentive to peripheral areas as a natural way to spot predators first. This makes it nearly impossible to track across a page of print, staying focused on small areas of print. Is this an exception or typical?

To find out, psychiatrist Wayne London switched the lighting in three classrooms at a Vermont elementary school. For the test, half had regular fluorescent bulbs and the other half had bulbs that simulated natural light (full-spectrum lights). The students in the full-spectrum classes missed 65 percent fewer school days from illness. Why? The regular fluorescent lighting has a flickering quality and barely audible hum that are scarcely noticeable but very powerful. Apparently the brain reacts to that visual-auditory stimulus by raising the cortisol levels in the blood and causing the eyes to blink excessively, both indicators of stress. In another study, elementary school children in rooms with the natural and full-spectrum lighting missed fewer school days and reported better moods (Edelston 1995).

Using classroom computers or watching videos also may be stressful for the eyes. It's tough on all ages but for a different reason when students are young. Their eyeballs are very soft and can get distorted by the continual near focusing, which is harder on the eyes than the more relaxed, distant vision. Neurophysiologist Dee Coulter says the task of keeping the eyes focused on a flat backlit screen is stressful (McGregor 1994). Many children spend up to five hours a day watching television, playing video games, or using a computer. As a result, adolescents and teenagers need glasses years earlier than they used to, Coulter says.

Social situations can be a source of stress, too. While stress hormones like cortisol are commonly released during stress, serotonin levels are affected, too. Diminished serotonin levels have been linked to violent and aggressive behaviors. For example, students who are "top dog" in their home life and just "one of many" in a classroom become more impulsive. Some of these students suddenly flourish when given roles like a team leader. Studies suggest that classroom status or social hierarchies can and do change the brain's chemistry. This makes a good case for the importance of changing roles often to ensure everyone has a chance to lead and follow.

Another source of environmental stress is the fact that our predictions rarely match reality. For adults, it's a day full of dissatisfaction with noise, erratic drivers, broken copy machines, colleagues who forget their promises, and computer glitches. It's no different for students. A typical schoolday is filled with expectations and disappointments, projects that don't work out, scores that are lower than usual, and classmates who don't act the way predicted. All of these "glitches" can be a source of stress. The brain often reacts to these as threats. What is the solution? Provide predictability through school and classroom rituals. A predictable event like a graded paper returned when promised or a peer cheer for celebration sets the unsettled brain at ease (Calvin 1996).

Some stress is not necessarily bad for learning. At Stanford University, Seymour Levine showed that young rats exposed to stressful shock experiences performed better as adults than the nonstressed controls (Thompson 1993). But the rats were not being asked to write a research paper. Those studies remind us that the military is well known for purposely creating stressful environments. Navy and Marine boot camps demand an endless list of perfectly executed chores. To force recruits to meet the standards, threats of physical retribution are commonplace (push-ups, laps, extra duties). But all this purposeful stress is for a good reason: Actual combat is both stressful and threatening. More important, the recruits are rarely asked to think creatively, which is impaired by stress. In short, for most learning conditions, low to moderate levels of stress are best. High stress or threat has no place in schools.

Threat and Learning

It should be noted that outwardly we all respond to potential threats differently. Some dismiss them, while others consider them a challenge and rise to the occasion. For others, they're devastating. However, the brain responds to threats in predictable ways. The moment a threat is detected, the brain jumps into high gear (see fig. 6.2).

The amygdala is at the center of all our fear and threat responses (LeDoux 1996). It focuses our attention and receives immediate direct inputs from the thalamus, sensory cortex, hippocampus, and frontal lobes. Neural projections (bundles of fibers) from the amygdala then activate the entire sympathetic system. Normally, it triggers the

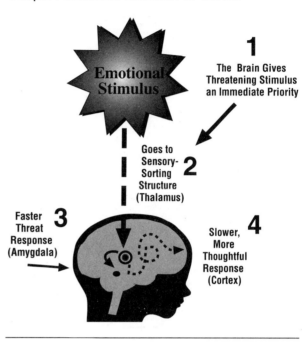

FIGURE 6.2

Simple Functional Reaction to Threat

release of adrenaline, vasopressin, and cortisol. These immediately change the way we think, feel, and act. Figure 6.3 summarizes the more detailed biological pathways of stress and threats.

Alan Rozanski reported in the *New England Journal of Medicine* that even harsh comments and sarcasm can trigger heart irregularities in patients predisposed to them (Rozanski 1988). New research reveals that threatening environments can even trigger chemical imbalances. Serotonin is the ultimate modulator of our emotions and subsequent behaviors. When serotonin levels fall, violence often rises. Not only can these imbalances trigger impulsive, aggressive behavior, but they also can lead to a lifetime of violence.

Students who have had early and constant childhood exposure to threat and high stress, particularly those who have come from families of vio-

FIGURE 6.3

Complex Pathways to Threat Response

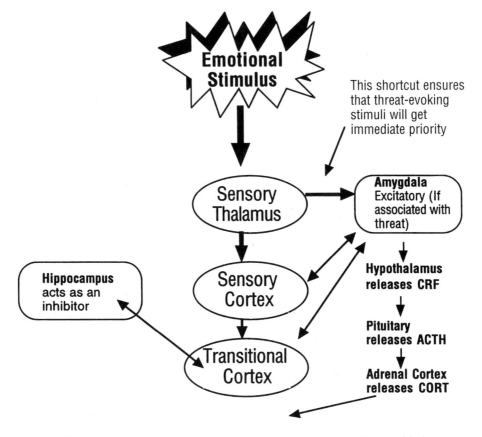

The result is that the body is now flush with chemical responses that enable it to fight, freeze, or flee. The measurable residue from this single biochemical response can last up to 48 hours.

lence, are often the ones for whom it is the most difficult to gain attention. Their vision and voice shift constantly, scanning the room for potential predators or "prey." They often swing or swat at other students as a way of establishing "rank." This territorialism is the source of the comments some kids make to others: "Don't look at me that way!" What they're doing is fending off potential problems. Their brains' receptor sites have adapted to a

survival-oriented behavior. While this behavior makes for frustrated teachers, it makes perfect sense to the student whose life seems to depend on it.

The list of possible threats for students is endless. Threats may exist in the student's home, on the way to school, in the hallways, and in the classroom. Threats might include an overstressed parent who threatens with violence, a loss of privileges at school or at home, a boyfriend or girlfriend who threatens to break up the relationship, or a bully who barks harsh words in the hallways. In the classroom, it could be a rude classmate or an unknowing teacher who threatens a student with humiliation, detention, or embarrassment before peers. Any of these events, and a thousand others, can put the brain on alert. It can't be repeated enough: Threats activate defense mechanisms and behaviors that are great for survival but lousy for learning.

Threats carry other costs. You get predictable, knee-jerk behaviors when the brain senses any threat that induces helplessness. Survival always overrides pattern-detection and complex problem solving. Students are less able to understand connections or detect larger levels of organization. This fact has tremendous implications for learning. Learning narrows to the memorization of isolated facts. Learners with lower stress can put together relationships, understand broad underlying theories, and integrate a wider range of material. Stress, threat, and induced learner helplessness must be removed from the environment to achieve maximum learning (see fig. 6.4).

FIGURE 6.4

Impact of Stress on Learning Performance

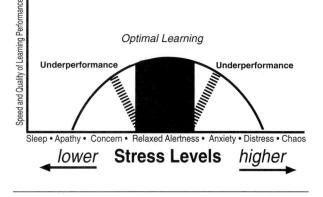

Learned Helplessness

Contrary to a *temporary* unmotivating state, learned helplessness is a chronic and devastating condition. It's often overdiagnosed, but it's nonetheless worthy of significant discussion. We see its symptoms in student comments like, "I'm stupid (or unlucky), so why bother?" Students demonstrate nearly complete apathy and persistent passivity. Learned helplessness is fairly rare in most classrooms, but when it occurs, it's quite discouraging. In order to "qualify" as learned helplessness, the following conditions have usually occurred.

• **Trauma.** The student was in a circumstance involving an important uncontrollable event. Although the most common events are severe threat or trauma, learned helplessness will result even if the uncontrollable event is positive or neutral (Peterson, Maier, and Seligman 1993). The event could be verbal, physical, or psychological. What does *not* qualify would be a teacher politely telling a student to quiet down or there will be a private discussion after class. What does often qualify is a bully in the hallways, an abusive home-life, or an insensitive teacher who embarrasses or humiliates a student in front of classmates. Under some conditions, the trauma can happen second-hand. For example, when there's a shooting at a school, counseling teams often need to help students who witnessed the trauma.

• **Lack of Control.** The student must have had the experience of *no control* over the traumatic threat and no skills in handling it. An example is the student who is put down harshly in class and feels immobilized by the embarrassment. That's different from the case of an abusive parent, where the student develops skills to deal with the problem and copes by fighting back, getting help, or running away. In that case the student realized the danger and made proactive choices. Some argue that asking students to accomplish tasks for which they lack the resources can also contribute to immobilization.

- **Decision.** The student must have made a paralyzing decision to explain the event and his or her reaction to it. Usually it takes the form of "I can't do anything right" or "I'm to blame" or "I'm bad luck." These conclusions are the precursor to forming such a negative expectation about the future that the result is no effort. These conclusions can also originate from repeated teacher criticisms like, "You're hopeless" or "You just don't try" (Peterson et al. 1993).

Which students are most susceptible to the condition of learned helplessness? The at-risk learners—those who come from threatening home lives and exhibit aggressive street survival behaviors in the classroom—may be most likely to be affected. This notion suggests that we might take a new look at the so called "lack of motivation" in the discouraged learner. The kids at school who *seem* to be the most able to deal with failure, students who are outgoing and verbal, may in fact, be the ones most unable to deal with it.

The Biology of Learned Helplessness

Here, the evidence is pervasive: Certain traumas can literally rewire the brain. The resulting stresses on students from lack of control "are typically so potent that they alter the activity of almost every neurotransmitter in some particular brain region and some neurotransmitter in almost every brain region," say Peterson and colleagues (1993). Right now, scientists have collected a great deal of "prob-

able biological suspects" yet still don't have the collective "gang." It's as if they know the notes but not the whole symphony. When a serious condition is present, intervention is necessary. Some students can be helped with prescription drugs, either stimulants or depressants.

A series of telling animal experiments (Maier and Geer 1968) illuminates the seriousness of lack of control. Dogs were placed in separate cages. They were given mild shocks through the grid floor, with no chance to escape. After their resignation became chronic, the shock was eliminated on half the cage. The dog was then dragged across to the safe area to let it feel the altered grid and see the light indicating safety. But the dog went right back to the shocked side and curled up in fear again. This is similar to a student who has learned to fail and simply won't even try.

How long do you think it took to get the dog to reengage actively in choice-making again? Five or 10 draggings? "After 30 to 50 such draggings, the dogs began to respond on their own," say Peterson and colleagues (1993). If you think humans are different, think again. When the brain's been rewired by experience, lives are changed. To see for yourself, visit a shelter for abused women. Or, visit most high schools and you'll see many laid-back "I don't care and it doesn't matter" kids. Unknowingly, teachers often give up on these students after 5 or 10 positive attempts. In fact, students who have learned to be helpless may need dozens of positive choice trials before becoming mobilized again. The brain must rewire itself to change the behavior.

Amazingly, a single exposure to trauma can produce changes to receptor sites in the brain. Remember, though, it's the issue of control, which is at the heart of learned helplessness, that has powerful biological consequences. If the student is in a traumatic situation and he makes choices, the condition will not occur, regardless of the outcome. This may be why, time and again, educational reformists have pushed the notion of student control. At a typical school, nearly every decision, from length of time on learning to whom to work with, is dictated and managed outside student control.

The Results of Learned Helplessness

What conclusions can be drawn from these biological changes? Two researchers P. Villanova and C. Peterson (cited in Peterson et al. 1993) analyzed 132 studies of learned helplessness that included several thousand human subjects. Part of the analysis compared human effects versus animal effects. The study notes, "[C]alculations suggest that the effect in people may be even stronger than the analogous effect in animals. . . ." (p. 107). Human experience with uncontrollable events disrupts performance at test tasks. Impaired problem solving is only the tip of the iceberg. The words the authors used to describe the impact were not trivial: they were "moderate" and "robust." In "researcher language," these words indicate compelling data. The suggestion is that we might take strong steps to reduce the occurrence of learned helplessness conditions and be proactive in dealing with it.

The emotional responses invoked in the subjects vary from anxiety to anger to depression. Humans who were stimulated to helplessness often became anxious, depressed, and restless, too. Trice (1982) found that exposure to helplessness increased a liking for hostile, as opposed to innocent, humor. You may have noticed that some of

your colleagues or students use excessive sarcasm and make hurtful comments to others. Students can be made helpless by being asked to work (even as a group) on tasks that can't be solved. This is an example of where the learned helplessness does not require an initial traumatic event (Peterson et al. 1993). Fortunately, specific strategies can reduce stress, eliminate threat, and head off learned helplessness.

Practical Suggestions

There are two approaches for reducing stress for students. One is to manage the conditions that can induce it, and the other is to use personal strategies that mediate and release it. Help students learn about what induces stress and what to do about it. Teach them stress management techniques like time management, breathing, the role of down time, relationships skills, and getting peer support. In the classroom, stress might be released through drama, peer support, games, exercise, discussions, and celebrations. Physical exercise triggers the release of a brain-derived neurotropic factor (BDNF) that enhances neural communication, elevates mood, and assists in long-term memory formation (Kinoshita 1997). A neurotropic factor is any agent that affects brain functioning. These include internal factors like hormones or external agents like caffeine or valium.

Work on the following three variables: threats from outside of class, threats from other students, and threats from yourself. You have little control on the outside environment, so be sure to establish a start of class transition time for students. It allows them to shift gears from the possibly dangerous outside world (a bully in the hallway, fights on the way to school, threats on the way to class). The transition time might include something physical: stretching, dance, manipulatives, a game, or a walk. It could be interpersonal, such as discussion with a small or large group or a neighbor. Finally, it might be personal, including journal writing, reflection, and creative writing.

Reduce threats from other students in class by setting up clear expectations about classroom behavior. Role model appropriate emotional intelligence. Discuss and use conflict resolution strategies. Follow through and enforce classroom rules. Never tolerate students threatening or hurting one another. Talk about what language is appropriate to use in school. Let students role play acceptable and inappropriate behaviors. Encourage the use of partners, work groups, and teams. Change them every three to six weeks to ensure everyone has a chance to meet and work with others in a variety of leadership and support roles.

It takes special vigilance to reduce threats. Avoid maintaining unrealistic deadlines by simply asking partway through an activity, "How many could use another few minutes?" Or, "How many of you think the one week due date is realistic?" Ask for what you want without adding a threat on the end. Instead of saying, "Kenny, keep it down, or I'll have to ask you to stay after," say, "Kenny, we're short on time today. Can you keep it down, please?" Never threaten misbehaviors with trips to the office. Either send someone or don't. Involve students in the class disciplining so that peers can help with the process.

Also avoid finger-pointing. Help students locate key resources like materials and work partners. Help students set specific, realistic, and measurable goals. Finally, ask students what is getting

in their way of learning. Sometimes it's a second language, a learning style, or even the student sitting next to them. As the teacher and adult, you're not saying to students you'll do anything they ask. However, it's important to show a willingness to listen and learn from them. As you include them in your planning, their participation and morale goes up and their requests for change will become more reasonable.

Several strategies are effective for reducing the impact of learned helplessness. Fortunately, the destructive effects often go away with time, say Young and Allin (1986). How much time depends on many factors including how often the stressor is retriggered and if any intervening "therapy" is administered. It can vary from a few days to several years. It's critical that educators recognize the situation early. Why? Surprisingly, students can be "immunized" against the possibility of learned helplessness (Altmaier and Happ 1985). The process is simple, but not easy.

Help students see the connections between their actions and the outcomes. Simply provide them with rich experiences of choice in school, particularly under stressful situations. If an impending test is becoming paralyzing, turn it into a "teachable" moment. Explain to the students how our bodies often react to stress. Give them ways to de-stress as well as options and resources for reaching their academic objectives. Visualization, managing negative self-talk, and test-taking strategies can be helpful. Students might need to know how to better manage their time, find information in the media center, or arrange to spend time with a study buddy.

Also, encourage students to explore alternative possibilities to explain a seemingly simple failure. Finally, put them in situations where they can literally relearn to mobilize themselves in the face of threat. Team activities and sports can contribute, as can theater or drama with public performances. For many students, the Outward Bound type challenge or ropes courses provide a great vehicle to learn to choose in the face of perceived threat.

Biology is giving us another way to approach some of the persistent problems educators face.

The role of excess stress helps us understand why so many students have problems with discriminating between what's important and what's not. Stress contributes to more illness, poor pattern recognition, and a weaker memory. The impact of threat reminds us to be careful. We can't afford to allow environmental threats, and we certainly must eliminate our own threatening behaviors and policies.

7 Motivation and Rewards

Nearly all educators deal with the issue of motivation. In fact, in the first few weeks of school, teachers often mentally group students into the categories of "motivated" and "unmotivated." The rest of the school year usually plays out these early perceptions of who is "ready to learn" and who isn't. A slew of tools, strategies, and techniques are marketed to a hungry audience of frustrated educators who work with "hard to reach" or perpetually "unmotivated" students.

Does our new understanding of the brain tell us anything about learner motivation? Is there really such a thing as an unmotivated learner? Why are some learners intrinsically motivated? And what does brain research tell us about using rewards? While the previous chapter focused on the role of stress and threat, it also highlighted chronic demotivation: the condition called learned helplessness. This chapter focuses on *temporary* motivation difficulties, the role of rewards, and developing intrinsic motivation.

Students and Motivation

The popularity of behaviorism in the 1950s and 1960s inspired a generation of educators to pursue rewards as a teaching strategy. We knew very little about the brain at that time, and rewards seemed cheap, harmless, and often effective. But there was more to the use of rewards than most educators understood. Surprisingly, much of the original research by Watson and Skinner was misinterpreted.

For example, the stimulus-response rewards popularized by behaviorism were effective only for simple physical actions. But schools often try to reward students for solving challenging cognitive problems, writing creatively, and designing and completing projects. There's an enormous difference in how the human brain responds to rewards for simple and complex problem-solving tasks. Short-term rewards can temporarily stimulate simple physical responses, but more complex behaviors are usually impaired, not helped, by rewards (Deci, Vallerand, Pelletier, and Ryan 1991, Kohn 1993).

In addition, the behaviorists made a flawed assumption: that learning is primarily dependent on a reward. In fact, rats—as well as humans—will consistently seek new experiences and behaviors with no perceivable reward or impetus. Experimental rats responded positively to simple novelty. Presumably, novelty-seeking could lead to new sources of food, safety, or shelter, thus enhancing species preservation. Choice and control over their environment produced more social and less aggressive behaviors (Mineka, Cook, and Miller 1984). Is it possible that curiosity or the mere pursuit of information can be valuable by itself? Studies confirm that this happens, and humans are just as happy to seek novelty (Restak 1979).

We have all looked for solutions to "motivate" learners. The long-term promise of better grades, pleasing others, graduation, and future employment are common "hooks." Short term, teachers offer choice, privileges, and getting out on time or early. These kinds of rewards seem to work with some, but not all, students. A study of 849 Los Angeles County 8th graders found that they scored 13 percent higher when offered $1 for every correct answer on a national math exam. This study suggests, among other things, that some students may actually know the material but be unmotivated to demonstrate it, according to study researcher Harold O'Neill (Colvin 1996).

A student can be momentarily in an apathetic state, or the demotivation may be chronic and debilitating. It takes a bit of detective work to make the distinction between the two. If the student goes in and out of "motivating" states and occasionally engages in learning, it's probably a temporary condition. This state has an enormous array of possible causes, but the solutions are relatively easy. Learned helplessness, the more chronic and severe demotivation, is quite different. (It was addressed in the previous chapter.)

Temporary Demotivation

Students who make it to school each day have demonstrated a certain amount of motivation. After all, they've made it to class while the truly unmotivated students are still in bed or anyplace else but school. That's why there are very few truly unmotivated students. The students you see may look like school is the last place they want to be, but at least they've made it to your class. And, most likely, they are *temporarily* unmotivated. Why? There are three primary reasons.

The first has to do with associations from the past, which can provoke a negative or apathetic state. These memory associations may be stored in the amygdala in the middle of the brain area

(LeDoux 1996). When they're triggered, the brain acts as if the incident were occurring in the moment. The same chemical reactions are triggered, and adrenaline, vasopressin, and ACTH are released into the bloodstream from the adrenal glands.

A teacher's voice, tone, or gestures may remind a student of a previous, disliked teacher. Past failures may trigger such feelings, as can memories of consistently failing a subject or having an embarrassing or "catastrophic" downfall in a class. An original significant threat can be retriggered by a much smaller incident (Peterson, Maier, and Seligman 1993).

A second reason is more present-time and environmental. Students can feel unmotivated in the face of unsuitable learning styles, a lack of resources, language barriers, a lack of choice, cultural taboos, fear of embarrassment, a lack of feedback, poor nutrition, prejudice, poor lighting, bad seating, the wrong temperature, fear of failure, a lack of respect, irrelevant content, and a host of other possibilities (Wlodkowski 1985). Each of these can be dealt with as the symptoms indicate. If students are visual learners, they will do better the more that they can see, look at, and follow with their eyes. If students can't understand the teacher's language, they'll do better when the teacher gives strong nonverbal communications or when they work with others in a cooperative group approach.

A third factor in the student's motivation is his or her relationship with the future. This includes the presence of clear, well-defined goals (Ford 1992). The learner's content beliefs ("I have the ability to learn this subject") and context beliefs ("I have the interest and resources to succeed in *this* class with *this* teacher") also are critical. These goals and beliefs create states that release powerful brain chemicals. Positive thinking engages the left frontal lobe and usually triggers the release of pleasure chemicals like dopamine as well as natural opiates, or endorphins. This self-reward reinforces the desired behavior.

Students in any of the three categories above are simply in a temporary unmotivated state. States are a snapshot of the mind-body in one moment: your brain's chemical balance, body temperature, posture, eye pattern, heartbeat, EEG, and a host of other measures. Because anyone can go into a plethora of states at any time (happy, hungry, anxious, curious, satisfied), the state called apathy may simply be one of many very appropriate responses to the environment. After all, we all go in and out of thousands of states per day. Our states change with what we eat, humidity, fatigue, special events, good or bad news, success, and failure. In the classroom, the teacher who understands the importance of states can be quite effective. Apathy often disappears with a simple engaging activity, listening or sharing, or the use of music or group activities.

Rewards and the Brain

Dean Wittrick, head of the Division of Educational Psychology at the University of California at Los Angeles (UCLA), says that today's classroom instruction is based on a flawed theory. "For a long time, we've assumed that children should get an immediate reward when they do something right," he said. "But the brain is much more complicated than most of our instruction; it has many systems operating in parallel" (p. 2). The brain is perfectly satisfied to pursue novelty and curiosity, embrace relevance, and bathe in the feedback from successes. He suggests extended applications of projects and problem solving where the process is more important than the answer. That's the real reward, he says (Nadia 1993).

Yet the old paradigm of behaviorism told us that to increase a behavior, we simply need to reinforce the positive. If there's a negative behavior exhibited, we ought to ignore or punish it. This is the "outside-in" point of view. It's as if we are looking at the student as the subject of an experiment. This approach says that if demotivation is an established condition, then there are causes and symptoms. This way of understanding classroom behavior seemed to make sense for many. But our understanding of motivation and behavior has changed. Tokens, gimmicks, and coupons no longer make sense when compared with more attractive alternatives.

Neuroscientists take a different view of rewards. First, the brain makes its own rewards. They are called opiates, which are used to regulate stress and pain. These opiates can produce a natural high, similar to morphine, alcohol, nicotine, heroin, and cocaine. The reward system is based in the brain's center, the hypothalamic reward system (Nakamura 1993). The pleasure-producing system lets you enjoy a behavior, like affection, sex, entertainment, caring, or achievement. You might call it a long-term survival mechanism. It's as if the brain says, "That was good; let's remember that and do it again!" Working like a thermostat or personal trainer, your limbic system ordinarily rewards cerebral learning with good feelings on a daily basis. Students who succeed usually feel good, and that's reward enough for most of them. Figure 7.1 summarizes the brain's internal reward system.

Does all of this mean that *external* rewards are also good for the brain? The answer is no. That's because the brain's internal reward system varies from one student to the next. You'd never be able to have a fair system. How students respond depends on genetics, their particular brain chemistry, and life experiences that have wired their brains in a unique way. Rewards work as a complex system of neurotransmitters binding to receptor sites on neurons. These sites act like ports for the docking of ships. Here, the neurotransmitters will either deliver an excitatory message to a NMDA (N-methyl-D-aspartate) receptor site or an inhibitory message to a GABA (gamma-amino-butyric acid) receptor. Without these "on" and "off" switches in the brain, the brain cells would fire indiscriminately. That would give all life experiences the same weight, and learning would be either impaired dramatically or nearly impossible. Most teachers have found that the same external reward is received differently by two different students. However, when a learning experience is positive, nearly all students will respond favorably in their unique biological ways. That makes rewards unequal from the start.

Steven Hyman of Harvard Medical School says "genetic susceptibility runs through the reward system" (cited in Kotulak 1996, p. 114). But researchers are unsure to what degree. Life experiences play an even more important role. Bruce Perry at the University of Chicago says that early childhood experiences that involve violence, threat, or significant stress actually rewire the brain. To survive, these brains have usually developed more receptor sites for noradrenaline. Behaviors include overarousal, strong attention to nonverbal clues, and aggressiveness. But in a classroom, there's no reward for displaying impulsive behaviors, threatening others, or interpreting nonverbals as aggressive. These students' brains are not

FIGURE 7.1

The Brain's Internal Reward System

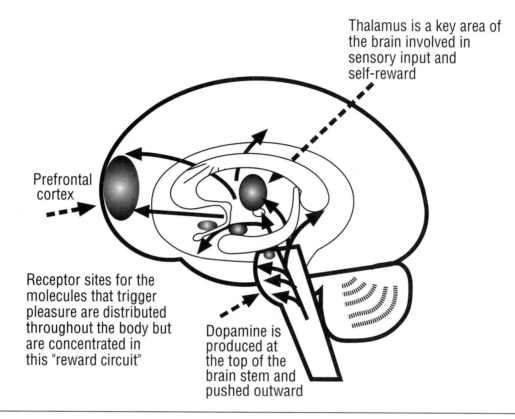

Thalamus is a key area of the brain involved in sensory input and self-reward

Prefrontal cortex

Receptor sites for the molecules that trigger pleasure are distributed throughout the body but are concentrated in this "reward circuit"

Dopamine is produced at the top of the brain stem and pushed outward

rewarded by the satisfaction of completing homework. They have learned to thrive just by surviving. The discipline strategies used by most teachers will fall short unless they understand why such students behave as they do. They will thrive when put in multiple team and cooperative roles where they can be both a leader and follower the same day. They also need emotional literacy skills in reading nonthreatening nonverbals.

From a social and educational context, rewards have already been studied and, to a large degree, rejected as a motivating strategy (Kohn 1993). But educators disagree on what constitutes a reward. A useful definition is that rewards need two ele-

ments: predictability and market value. Let's say a teacher's class puts on a play for the school and parents once a year. At the end of the play, the audience offers a standing ovation. The kids come off stage, and the proud teacher announces that she's taking everyone out for pizza. Is that a reward? No, it's a celebration. Had she said to the students right before the opening curtain, "Do well and you'll all get pizza," it would have been a reward. Pizza, candy, stickers, privileges, and certificates all have market value. Research suggests that students will want them each time the behavior is required, they'll want an increasingly valuable reward, and rewards provide little or no lasting pleasure. Amabile (1989) has documented extensively how the use of rewards damages intrinsic motivation. While most schools know that even grades are themselves a form of rewards, only a select few have moved to a credit/no credit system.

Promoting Intrinsic Motivation

While it's been fashionable to label students as "motivated" or "unmotivated," the reality is much different. Most students are already intrinsically motivated; it's just that the motivation is very context dependent. The same student who is lethargic in a traditional math class can become quite energetic when figuring out paycheck deductions from her first job. Thus, we can infer that we have been looking in the wrong places for motivation.

This may lead many educators to ask, "If we can't reward positive behaviors, how do we motivate learners?" Maybe a better question to ask is, "When students are motivated, what's going on in the brain?" Or, "What conditions are present that foster that precious inner drive?" Researchers tell us that several factors are present: compelling goals, positive beliefs, and productive emotions (Ford 1992). Any discussion about intrinsic motivation must also include the learner's natural search and subsequent construction for meaning. Meaning will be explored in a later chapter. While neuroscientists haven't yet figured out the biological correlates of goals and beliefs, we do know much more about the factor of emotions.

The emotions of stress and threat may either mobilize us or render us passive. On the positive side, several neurotransmitters are involved in natural, intrinsic motivation. If it's mild, cognitive motivation, we may see increased levels of norepinephrine, or dopamine. If it's stronger, more active motivation, it may be increased levels of the peptide vasopressin or adrenaline. The artificial manipulation of these chemicals often happens through medications and food. At school, teachers can do many things to encourage the release of those motivating chemicals. Figure 7.2 presents five key strategies to help students uncover their intrinsic motivation.

The first strategy is to eliminate threat. It takes time and a strong intent, but it's worth it. Some teachers have asked students to meet in small groups to brainstorm a list of the things that inhibit their learning. The groups could then discuss how some of the problems could be alleviated. Use an anonymous class survey to ask students what would make learning more potent and enjoyable.

Second, goal-setting (with some student choice) on a daily basis can provide a more focused attitude. Prepare students for a topic with "teasers" or personal stories to prime their interest. For example, "Today we're going to explore your body's own highway system for the movement of nutrients, the circulatory system. The last time you got sick, this system was part of the solution to getting better." This ensures that the content is relevant to them.

Third, influence positively in every way you can, symbolically and concretely, students' beliefs about themselves and the learning. This includes the use of affirmations, acknowledging student successes, positive nonverbals, teamwork, or positive posters.

Fourth, manage student emotions through the productive use of rituals, drama, movement, and celebration. Teach students how to manage their own emotions, too.

Finally, feedback is one of the greatest sources of intrinsic motivation. Set up learning that stu-

FIGURE 7.2

Practical Alternatives to Using Rewards

Eliminate Threat
Uncover problems
Add transition time
Avoid demands

Create Strongly Positive Climate
Acknowlegments
Rich Environment
Policies/Rituals
Relationship Building

Set Goals
Meaning-Making
Student Choices
Valid Reasons
Clear Purpose

Increase Feedback
Peers/Family
Projects
Computers
Self-Evaluation
Natural Results

Activate and Engage Positive Emotions
Drama, Music, Art
Celebrations, Service Work
Games/Win-Win Competition

dents can do with endless, self-managed feedback. A computer does this perfectly, but so do well-designed projects, group work, checklists, drama, peer editing, and rubrics.

The SuperCamp Model

One academic program incorporates all five of these suggestions. Co-founded by the author (Eric Jensen) and Bobbi DePorter, SuperCamp is a 10-day academic immersion program for students aged 12–22. Many students arrive at the program with a history of chronic demotivation. Yet long-term follow-up studies suggest that after attending for just 10 days, students become insatiable learners who improve grades, school participation, and self-esteem (Dryden and Vos 1994). SuperCamp has become a model for schools around the world by demonstrating how to bring out the best in kids.

The SuperCamp staff is thoroughly trained to eliminate threat from the camp environment. They ask the question, "What do kids experience and what is threatening to them?" As a result, it's quite exciting to see the elimination of threat in practice. You might want to get your staff together and brainstorm factors that might contribute to threat and high stress. Some of the likely sources are threatening comments, "score keeping" discipline strategies, sarcasm, unannounced "pop" quizzes, a lack of resources, unforgiving deadlines, and cultural or language barriers.

Create "emotional bridges" from students' worlds outside the classroom to the start of learning. Make the assumption (even though it won't always be true) that your students need transition time from their personal lives to the the academic lives and from one teacher to the next. You never know what happens out in the hallways. At the start of class, students could still be reeling from an insult, a break-up with a close friend, a fight, or the loss of something valuable. Using dependable activities that trigger specific, predictable states can be the perfect way to bridge into learning. Appropriate rituals keep the stress levels low and can even eliminate threat responses.

For example, each morning at SuperCamp starts with "getting ready to learn" time. These predictable, safe rituals include a morning walk with a partner, time with teammates to discuss personal problems, reviewing the previous day's learning, and stretching during morning physical activity. Such built-in transitions allow for the brain to change to the right chemical state needed for learning. It also allows everyone to "synchronize" their clocks to the same learning time. Follow-up studies indicate that this threat-reducing process works (DePorter and Hernacki 1992).

During the day at SuperCamp, high levels of novelty, movement, and choice enrich a highly relevant curriculum (how to run your own brain, problem solving, conflict resolution, and learning to learn). The end of the day follows the same routine as the start, almost in reverse. Closure rituals help students put learning from the day in its new cognitive-emotional place.

You might consider arrival and beginning rituals that include music fanfare, positive greetings, special handshakes, hugs, or sharing time. Certain songs can be used to bring students back from a break and let them know it's time to start up. (Music sure beats a bell!) Group and organizational rituals also help, such as team names, cheers, gestures, and games. Successful situational rituals include applause when learners contribute, a song to close or end something, affirmations, discussion, journal writing, cheers, self-assessment, and gestures. These opportunities to influence the affective side of learning make a strong case for longer teaching blocks at the secondary level. This way, a teacher can practice some of these strategies and still have adequate time for content.

The SuperCamp environment provides extensive opportunities for students to get personal and academic feedback. Students usually get this feedback 10 to 20 times a day though the purposeful use of sharing time, goal setting, group work, question-and-answer time, observation of others, and journals. Teachers who specifically design their learning to have dozens of methods of learner-generated feedback—not one or two—find that motivation soars. Peer feedback is more motivating and useful than teacher feedback in getting lasting results (Druckman and Sweets 1988).

The whole issue of learned helplessness is dealt with at SuperCamp in a dramatic way. Studies indicate that the best way to treat the condition is to use multiple trials of compelling or "forced" positive choice (Peterson et al. 1993). In other words, if you always let a student do whatever he or she wants, he'll often do nothing. At camp, the double-edge sword of strongly bonded teamwork and an Outward Bound style "ropes course" with a particular goal usually does the trick. On the all-day course, students are put in the position of having to make dramatic choices. "Do I climb another step up this 50-foot ladder? Do I jump off this trapeze bar? Do I trust others and fall backwards into their arms?" These decisions are made over and over throughout the day. They help students realize that they *do* matter to others and that they *can* choose good decisions and get support from their team. You most likely won't be able to use a "ropes course" with your students, but drama, goal setting, physical activities, and classroom responsibility have proven helpful.

Practical Suggestions

Temporary demotivation is common and should ordinarily not be considered a crisis. The causes could be many, and the solutions are fairly easy to administer. They include better staff training in the areas of cultural awareness, learning styles, and state management, and more resources such as peer help, computers, and criteria lists. Also helpful are reduced language barriers, greater use of student choice, and elimination of any kind of embarrassment or use of sarcasm. In addition, take the time to provide more quantity, variety, and quality of feedback and encourage better nutrition. It also helps if students generate clear, well-defined goals and learn the skills of positive thinking.

Researchers are developing better tools to understand the inner workings of the motivated brain. In whole, the collected research leads us to understand that part of the problem is the way we treat students. They are not factory workers who need to be prodded, cajoled, and motivated by bribes, management, or threats. Instead of asking, "How can I motivate students?", a better question would be, "In what ways is the brain naturally motivated from within?" Can you encourage better learning this way? The answer is a definite yes, and educators around the world already are succeeding with it every day.

8 Emotions and Learning

The cognitive side of learning usually gets a great deal of attention, but a tugging undercurrent persists. It is the domain of emotions, the so-called affective side of learning. We all know it's there, but it's commonly thought of as a distraction to learning. In fact, some still believe that learning and emotions are at opposite ends of the spectrum. It's time for all of us to catch up on the research.

Biologically, emotions are not only very current science, but also very important science. Neuroscientists are now breaking new ground in mapping out this important learning component. The affective side of learning is the critical interplay between how we feel, act, and think. There is no separation of mind and emotions; emotions, thinking, and learning are all linked. This chapter makes the case that emotions have an important and rightful place in learning and in schools.

Western Culture and Emotions

Western culture has had a peculiar attitude about human emotion. Though we acknowledge that emotions exist, they have always held lower court.

Literature has portrayed the world of emotions as erratic, flighty, uncontrollable, whimsical, and even sinister. The stable, dependable, "scientific" path has been that of reason and logic.

But what if what we considered logical was actually emotional? What if it was *more* rational to include emotions in our thinking and decision making? For many, the mere thought is outrageous. Science is about facts, not feelings. As a result, most scientists, particularly biologists and neuroscientists, considered it professional suicide to study emotions as a serious topic. "Better left to the psychiatrists" was the prevailing view.

In fact, you might say emotions have been the black sheep of the brain family. Peter Stearns says our society has gone "anti-intensity," trumpeting a new low emotionality; otherwise, you're portrayed as being "out of control" (Atlas 1996). This view may have been brought on by the media's portrayal of violent individuals as lacking self-discipline. But what are the scientific links between emotions and learning? Could it actually be smarter to organize learning around emotions?

Emotions Make the Mainstream

While several researchers made references to, and even did occasional studies on, emotions, no one made it a career path for the longest time. It remained that way until the mid-1980s. Then, five highly respected neuroscientists—Joseph LeDoux of New York University, Candace Pert of Georgetown University Medical Center, Jerome Kagan of Harvard, and Antonio Damasio and Hanna Damasio of the University of Iowa—emerged with important research. Each has made meaningful contributions that helped change the way we think of emotions.

Emotions drive attention, create meaning, and have their own memory pathways (LeDoux 1994). You can't get more related to learning than that. Kagan says, "The rationalists who are convinced that feelings interfere with the most adaptive choices have the matter completely backwards. A reliance on logic alone, without the capacity to feel . . . would lead most people to do many, many more foolish things" (1994, p. 39). The old way of thinking about the brain is a separateness of mind, body, and emotions. That idea's history, Antonio Damasio reminds us: "The body . . . may constitute the indispensable frame of reference for . . . the mind" (1994, p. xvi); and in fact, "reduction in emotion may constitute an equally important source of irrational behavior" (p. 53). Emotion helps reason to focus the mind and set priorities. Many researchers now believe that emotion and reason are not opposites. For example, our logical side says, "Set a goal." But only our emotions get us passionate enough even to care enough to act on that goal.

One of the original scholars to construct the theory of emotional intelligence, Jack Mayer believes that emotions convey information, just like data or logic. Psychology has been too atomized in the sense that it divided intelligence, motor behavior, and emotions into different areas, rather than considering the inseparable links among them (Marquis 1996, p. B-2). The popularity of the bestselling *Emotional Intelligence* (Goleman 1995) has raised emotions to an acceptable, if not reputable, level. Some are now calling it an entirely new discipline in neuroscience (Davidson and Sutton 1995). You never would have found this kind of scientific support for the role of emotions 10 years ago. What caused the change?

Three discoveries in the field of emotions have changed the way we think of them. First is the discovery of the physical pathways and priorities of emotions. Second are findings about the brain's chemicals involved in emotions. Third is a link between these pathways and chemicals to everyday learning and memory.

The first element gave emotions something "solid," some kind of grounded reality that we could measure. It was concrete information you could see in an autopsy or on a screen. The second discovery helped us understand the pervasive nature of emotions. The third was the researcher's jackpot: the critical link that our very survival is dependent on emotions.

The Measurement of Emotion

Neuroscientists usually separate emotions and feelings. Emotions are generated from biologically automated pathways. They are joy (pleasure), fear, surprise, disgust, anger, and sadness. Cross-cultural studies indicate that these six expressions are universal. The only emotions that researchers have found specific sites for in the brain are fear and pleasure. That's why the earlier, biologically linked models of learning were dominated by studies on threats and rewards. Feelings are different; they're our culturally and environmentally developed responses to circumstances. Examples include: worry, anticipation, frustration, cynicism, and optimism. Emotions are very real. When we say the emotions are involved, we have a vast array of highly specific and scientific ways to measure precisely what is happening, including skin responses, heart rate, blood pressure, and EEG activity. It's easy to get readings on a student's response

---

FIGURE 8.1

The Objective Nature of Emotions

We can use information from the autonomic (sweat glands, heart activity, blood pressure, and gastrointestinal); central (electrical activity of the brain's neurons); or sensorimotor systems (respiration, eye movements, etc.) to measure emotions.

SCR... skin conductance response
Pulse... heartbeats per minute
EGG... electrogastrography...gastrointestinal system measures
BP... blood pressure
BEAM... brain electrical activity mapping
SPR... skin-potential response
ERP... central nervous system, the event-related potentials
fMRI... functional magnetic resonance imaging
EEG... electroencephalography
BR... breathing rates
RCBF... regional cerebral blood flow
MT... muscle tension
HRPSA... heart rate power spectrum analysis
MEG... magnetoelectroencephalography
PET... position emission tomography, blood flow measurements
SC... skin color, flushed skin

---

to fear, but we don't yet have a way to measure feelings of sympathy, for example. Figure 8.1 shows information we can use to measure emotions.

The Pathways of Emotion

General feeling states and intense emotions of fear and pleasure take separate biological pathways in the brain (LeDoux 1996). (Fig. 8.2 summarizes the areas of the brain involved with emotion.) While feelings travel a circuitous, slower route throughout the body, the emotions always take the brain's "superhighways." In the mid-brain area, LeDoux (1992) found a bundle of neurons that lead directly from the thalamus to the amygdala. Some

FIGURE 8.2

Areas of the Brain Strongly Activated by Emotions

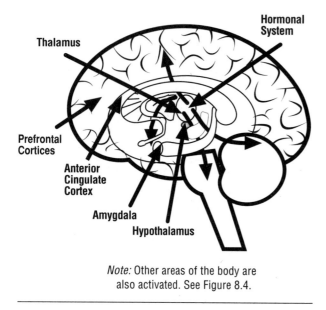

Note: Other areas of the body are also activated. See Figure 8.4.

information will get emotional priority before measured thinking takes place. Any experience that evokes threat or activates our brain's pleasure circuits activates specific neurons that respond only to these events.

In an emergency, prolonged evaluation may cost you your life. Any life-or-death situation needs immediate resources, not reflection and contemplation. This allows us to become, as Goleman suggests, "emotionally hijacked" by our responses (1995, Chapter 2). While our emotional system is acting independently, it's also acting cooperatively with our cortex. For example, a student who's getting threatening looks from another student may strike back at the perceived threat before even thinking about it. The teacher's "behavior improvement lecture" after the event usually does little to change the next "automatic" occurrence of hitting.

Students need to be taught emotional intelligence skills in a repetitive way that makes positive behaviors as automatic as negative ones. This point is particularly important because although today's students have no saber-toothed tigers to fight off, they have equivalent threats. These include fear of embarrassment, being a failure to their peers, or getting bullied in the hallway. Their brain has adapted to treat those emotional, psychological, and physical threats as if they are life-threatening.

According to Jeff Tooby of the University of California at Santa Barbara (Marquis 1996), the expression circuitry of emotion is widely distributed in our brain. While the old model linked the entire mid-brain (the limbic system) to emotions, the amygdala, an almond-shaped structure, seems most involved. There's no evidence that other areas of the so-called "limbic system" are heavily involved in direct emotions. That's why the phrase "limbic system" makes no sense according to LeDoux (1996).

The amygdala has 12 to 15 distinct emotive regions on it. So far, only two, the ones linked to fear, have been identified. Other emotions may be linked to other areas. The amygdala exerts a tremendous influence on our cortex. There are more inputs *from* the amygdala into the cortex than the reverse. Yet, information flows both ways. The design of these feedback circuits ensures that the impact of emotions will usually be greater. It becomes the weight to all our thoughts, biases, ideas, and arguments. It is in fact an emotional flavor that animates us, not a logical one. When classroom teachers evaluate student performance, it's all about how they feel about what they see and hear. The feelings strongly flavor the evaluation. We call it a professional opinion, but to say there's no emotion would be a case of serious denial.

Our emotions are our personalities and help us make most of our decisions. When researchers remove areas of the frontal lobe (the area of so-called highest intelligence), human performance in standard tests of intelligence usually drops very little. The removal is often necessary in the case of brain tumors that grow, then compress and kill nearby tissue. Generally patients can recover quite well and retain thinking skills (Damasio 1994, p. 42; Pearce 1992, p. 48). Removing the amygdala, however, is devastating. That destroys the capacities for creative play, imagination, key decision making, and the nuances of emotions that drive the arts, humor, imagination, love, music, and altruism. These are many of the qualities that we assign to those who make great contributions to our world. The genius of Quincy Jones, Martha Graham, Stephen Hawking, Eddie Murphy, and Mother Teresa are all examples of emotions driving creativity.

The Chemistry of Emotion

Brain chemicals are transmitted not only from the commonly cited axonal-synapse-dendrite reaction but also are dispersed to wide areas of the brain. The person who is depressed is often treated with Prozac, a medication that modulates serotonin levels. Caffeine boosts amine levels, which boosts alertness. When you experience a gut feeling, it's because the same peptides that are released in your brain are also lining your gastrointestinal tract. Memory is regulated by acetylcholine, adrenaline, and serotonin levels.

These active chemicals are pushed out from areas such as the medulla, adrenals, kidneys, and pons. This allows the chemicals of emotions to influence most of our behaviors. These chemicals linger and often dominate our system. That's why once an emotion occurs, it is hard for the cortex to simply shut it off. From choosing curriculum to monitoring the lunchroom, how we feel is usually how we act (fig. 8.3). The old paradigm was that our brain was managed by the physical connections made at the site of the synapse. But the newer, emerging understanding is that messenger molecules known as peptides are not only distributed throughout the brain and body, but exert a far greater influence on our behaviors than previously thought. Miles Herkenham of the National Institute of Mental Health says that 98 percent of all communication within the body may be through these peptide messengers (in Pert 1997, p. 139). This view implies a far greater role for the understanding and integration of emotions in learning.

The reason these states are so powerful is because they are produced and modulated throughout the body. Every cell has countless receptor sites on it for receiving information from other areas of the body; the bloodstream is the body's second nervous system! Figure 8.4 shows how ligands (the peptide messenger molecules) fit into receptor sites, transfer their information, and a new cell behavior begins. Multiply that by millions of cells, and a student simply feels differently.

Emotions as Mind-Body States

Emotions affect student behavior because they create distinct, mind-body states. A state is a moment composed of a specific posture, breathing rate, and chemical balance in the body. The presence or absence of norepinephrine, vasopressin, testosterone, serotonin, progesterone, dopamine, and dozens of other chemicals dramatically alters your frame of mind and body. How important are states

Figure 8.3

The Chemical Influences on Attention and Behavior

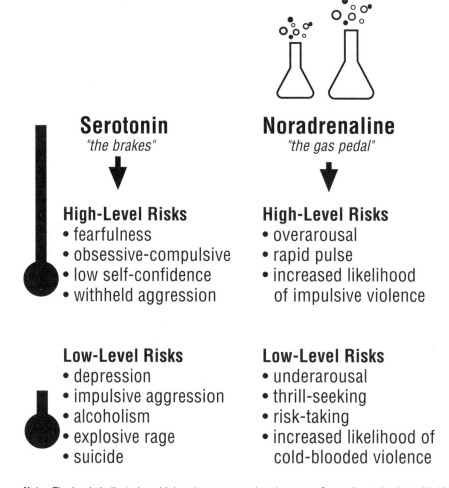

Serotonin
"the brakes"

High-Level Risks
• fearfulness
• obsessive-compulsive
• low self-confidence
• withheld aggression

Low-Level Risks
• depression
• impulsive aggression
• alcoholism
• explosive rage
• suicide

Noradrenaline
"the gas pedal"

High-Level Risks
• overarousal
• rapid pulse
• increased likelihood
  of impulsive violence

Low-Level Risks
• underarousal
• thrill-seeking
• risk-taking
• increased likelihood of
  cold-blooded violence

Note: *The levels indicated are high or low compared to the norm. Generally, males have 20-40% lower serotonin levels than females. Human behavior is complex, and there are other influencing factors besides chemical imbalances.*

to us? They are all that we have; they are our feelings, desires, memories, and motivations. A change of state is what your students use money for: They buy food to get out of the hunger state and buy Nike shoes to feel more confident or to be liked by classmates. They even buy drugs to change their state, either to feel better or to simply feel something. Educators need to pay attention to this. Teachers who help their students feel good about learning through classroom success, friendships, and celebrations are doing the very things the student brain craves.

FIGURE 8.4

How Emotions Influence the Learner: They Are the Body's Second Nervous System

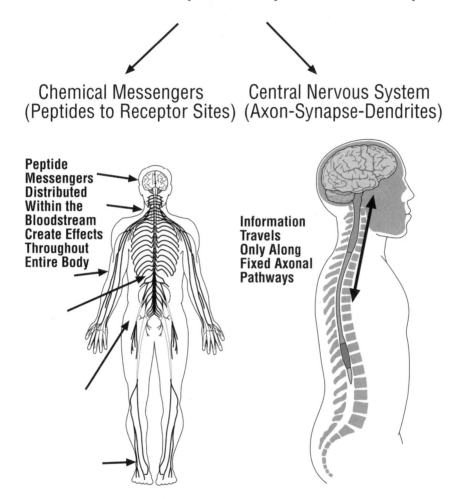

Chemical Messengers
(Peptides to Receptor Sites)

Peptide Messengers Distributed Within the Bloodstream Create Effects Throughout Entire Body

Central Nervous System
(Axon-Synapse-Dendrites)

Information Travels Only Along Fixed Axonal Pathways

Feeling states powerfully influence the learner's meaning-making, motivation, everyday behavior, and cognition. As an example, even if you like to go out dancing, if you're tired, you might pass on the opportunity.

Neurosurgeon Richard Bergland says, "[T]hought is not caged in the brain but is scattered all over the body" (Restak 1993, p. 207). He adds that he has little doubt the brain operates more like a gland than a computer. It produces hormones, is bathed in them, and is run by them. Emotions trigger the chemical changes that alter our moods, behaviors, and, eventually, our lives. If people and activities are the content in our lives, emotions are both the contexts and the values we hold. We simply cannot run a school without acknowledging emotions and integrating them into daily operations. Many schools do this already. They have pep rallies, guest speakers, poetry readings, community service efforts, storytelling, debates, clubs, sports, and dramatic arts.

Emotions, Learning, and Memory

For years we've been brainwashed into thinking it's our frontal lobes that give us our brilliant, "best of humanity" thoughts. While the frontal lobes allow us to elaborate on the details of our goals and plans, it's emotions that generate them and drive their execution in our lives (Freeman 1995, p. 89). That's why it's important to ask students to explain *why* they want to reach the goals they set. You might say, "Write down three good reasons why reaching your goals is important to you." Then, have the students share their responses with others. The reasons are the emotions behind the goals and the source of the energy to accomplish them (see fig. 8.5).

Emotions are a distillation of learned wisdom; the critical survival lessons of life are emotionally hardwired into our DNA. We have been biologically shaped to be fearful, worried, surprised, suspicious, joyful, and relieved, almost on cue. We must cease the long-standing habit of thinking of emotions as always irrational or having nothing to do with the ways we think. Emotions are a critical source of information for learning (LeDoux 1993). What if you ignored your feelings every time you did something dangerous or ill-advised? If you feel frustrated and tell off your boss, you might jeopardize your career very quickly. Fortunately, feelings

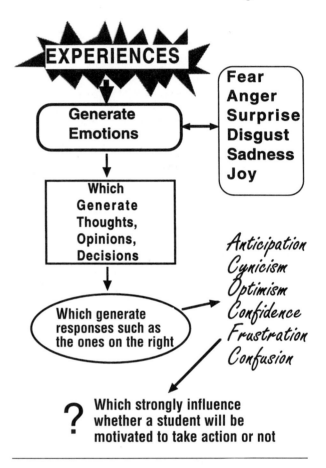

FIGURE 8.5

How Emotional States Affect Learning

of guilt or remorse are likely to prevent that. Students who feel tentative or afraid to speak in front of their peers are that way for a "logical" reason: to fail may cost them significant social status.

Making daily decisions based on emotions is not an exception; it's the rule. While extremes of emotion are usually harmful to our best thinking, a middle ground makes sense. Appropriate emotions speed up decision making enormously (Damasio 1994). If you're asked to join a colleague for lunch, you'll make your decision based on quick gut feelings: yes or no. To gather sufficient information might be rude or time consuming. Where are we going for lunch? What's the food like? Who else will be there? What's the agenda? Who's paying? Will it be fun? Who's driving? Is the car safe? When will we be back? Is there a better offer? It's far more useful, most of the time, to have a feeling about what to do next, then do it.

Emotions not only help us make better decisions faster, but we make better quality, value-based decisions. In fact, we make thousands of micro-decisions daily that shape our character as either on time or late, honest or sleazy, gossipy or noble, creative or unimaginative, and generous or stingy. Each of those decisions is made with a guiding hand—our values. All values are simply emotional states. If my value is honesty, then I feel badly when I'm dishonest. Conversely, I feel good when I do honest things. In a sense, our character is shaped by the conscience of our emotions. While too much or too little emotion is usually counterproductive, our everyday normal emotions are an important part of living.

While all of us acknowledge that we have emotions, few of us realize that they are not the cards at the game table but the table itself. Everything we experience has an emotional tone to it, from calm to rage, from pain to pleasure, and from relaxed to threatened. And, because emotions mediate our meaning, our emotions are, in fact, the framework for our day. Every day, how our day goes is how our emotions go. Even if you use a logic-driven rubric to evaluate every student's project, emotions still rule. On a bad day, your feelings about certain students or a particular rating criteria will lead you to rate one project as more creative, another as more organized, another as meeting the standards, and another as inadequate.

In addition, we remember that which is most emotionally laden. That happens because all emotional events receive preferential processing (Christianson 1992) and the brain is overstimulated when strong emotions are present. Emotions give us a more activated and chemically stimulated brain, which helps us recall things better. The more intense the amygdala arousal, the stronger the imprint (Cahill, Prins, Weber, and McGaugh 1994), says Goleman (1995). In fact, Larry Squire—a neurobiologist and memory expert at the University of California at San Diego—says that emotions are so important, they have their own memory pathways. James McGaugh, a neurobiologist at the University of California at Irvine, and fellow researchers agree. When emotions are suppressed or expressed in inappropriate ways, we get discipline problems. As teachers, we can purposely engage productive emotions. It's common for students to remember the death of a friend, a field trip, or a hands-on science experiment far longer than most lectures. Good learning does not avoid emotions, it embraces them.

Emotions researcher and prize-winning neuroscientist Candace Pert of Georgetown University Medical Center says that "when emotions are expressed . . . all systems are united and made whole. When emotions are repressed, denied, not allowed to be whatever they may be, our network pathways get blocked, stopping the flow of the vital feel-good unifying chemicals that run both our biology and our behavior" (Pert 1997, p. 273).

Practical Strategies

Triggering emotions randomly is counterproductive. In addition, extremes of emotion are generally counterproductive to school goals. A lack of emotion is just as dangerous as uncontrollable emotion. The old adage was, "First, get control of the students, then do the teaching." Today, neuroscientists might tell you to engage emotions appropriately at every chance you get. Engage emotions as a part of the learning, not as an add-on. You may have already used music, games, drama, or storytelling to engage emotions. Here are five more simple ways.

Role Model

Teachers ought to simply model the love of learning, and they should show enthusiasm about their job. For example, bring something with great excitement to class. Build suspense, smile, tell a true emotional story, show off a new CD, read a book, or bring an animal. Get involved in community work whether it's for a holiday, disaster relief, or ongoing service. Let students know what excites you.

Celebrations

Use acknowledgments, parties, high-fives, food, music, and fun. A celebration can show off student work in different ways. For example, when students are finished mind-mapping something, ask them to get up and show their poster-sized mind-map to eight other pairs of students. The goal is to find at least two things they like about it. As they carry around their mind-map, they point out things to students and they learn from their classmates. Play some celebration music, and everyone has a good time. Ideally, celebrations will be made "institutional" so students celebrate without a teacher prompt every time.

A Controversy

Setting up a controversy could involve a debate, dialogue, or an argument. Any time you've got two sides, a vested interest, and the means to express opinions, you'll get action! Have students prioritize a list by consensus, and you'll get emotions. Afterward, split up sides for a tug-of-war outside. Research indicates that when emotions are engaged right after a learning experience, the memories are much more likely to be recalled and accuracy goes up (McGaugh, Cahill, Parent, Mesches, Coleman-Mesches, and Salinas 1995). The debate could be in pairs of students, or turn it into an academic decathlon or game show. Theater and drama can create strong emotions: the bigger the production, the higher the stakes, the more the emotions engaged. For example, if your group volunteers to put on a schoolwide play, there are rehearsals, stress, fun, anxiety, anticipation, suspense, excitement, and relief.

Purposeful Use of Physical Rituals

Rituals in your class can instantly engage learners. Those rituals could include clapping patterns, cheers, chants, movements, or a song. Use these to announce arrival, departure, a celebration, and getting started on a project. Make the ritual fun and quick, and change it weekly to prevent boredom. Each time teams complete their tasks, they could give a team cheer. Or they could have a special cheer for each member upon arrival and another for the close of the day. Obviously, rituals should be age appropriate.

Introspection

The use of journals, discussion, sharing, stories, and reflection about things, people, and issues engages students personally. If there is a disaster in the news, ask students to write or talk about it. Current events or personal dramas work well, too.

If appropriate, students can share their thoughts with a neighbor or peer groups. Help students make personal connections to the work they do in class. For example, if students are writing journals, have them read "Letters to the Editor" in a local newspaper and discuss or even critique them. Students can choose an issue they are passionate about and submit letters to be printed.

Good learning engages feelings. Far from an add-on, emotions *are* a form of learning. Our emotions are the genetically refined result of life-times of wisdom. We have learned what to love, when and how to care, whom to trust, the loss of esteem, the exhilaration of success, the joy of discovery, and the fear of failure. This learning is just as critical as any other part of education. Many activities have powerful lifelong effects, yet there are few results to show on a daily scorecard. Emotions encompass one such area. Research supports the value of engaging appropriate emotions. They are an integral and invaluable part of every child's education.

9 Movement and Learning

In times of diminishing financial resources, educators must make hard choices. Do dance, theater, and physical education belong in the budget? Are they frills or fundamentals? What exactly does brain research tell us about the relationship between the body and mind?

For years it seemed that the educational and scientific communities believed that thinking was thinking and movement was movement, and never the twain would meet. Maverick scientists envisioned links between thinking and movement for decades—but with little public support. Today we know better. This chapter reveals the strong links between physical education, the arts, and learning.

Mind and Body

If we want to address drug education, second languages, diversity education, multiple intelligences, improving reading scores, reducing dropouts, encouraging girls in math and science, thematic instruction, and AIDS education, that's great. But what will we eliminate to make time for those things? Anything deemed a frill is likely to go first. For some short-sighted officials, that means physical education. Recent brain research tells us that's a mistake.

Part of the reason for the outdated separation of mind and body comes from simple observation. If the brain is in the head and the body is below the head, how could there be any links? What would happen if the cerebellum, an area most commonly linked to movement, turned out to be a virtual switchboard of cognitive activity? The first evidence of a linkage between mind and body originated decades ago with Henrietta Leiner and Alan Leiner, two Stanford University neuroscientists. Their research began what would eventually redraw "the cognitive map" (S. Richardson 1996).

The Leiners' work centered on the cerebellum, and they made some critical discoveries that spurred years of fruitful research. First, the cerebellum takes up just one-tenth of the brain by volume, but it contains *over half* of all its neurons. It has some 40 million nerve fibers, 40 times more than even the highly complex optical tract. Those fibers not only feed information from the cortex to the cerebellum, but they feed them back to the cortex. If this was only for motor function, why are the connections so powerfully distributed in both directions to all areas of the brain? In other words, this subsection of the brain—long known for its role in posture, coordination, balance, and movement—may be our brain's sleeping giant. (Fig. 9.1 shows the location of key areas of the brain involved in movement.)

In the past, the cerebellum was thought to merely process signals from the cerebrum and send them to the motor cortex. The mistake was in assuming the signals went only to the motor cortex. They don't (S. Richardson 1996, p. 100). The last place information is processed in the cerebellum,

FIGURE 9.1

Location of Key Brain Areas Involved in Movement

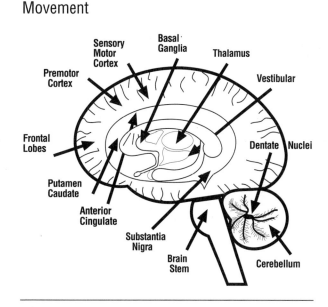

before it is sent to the cortex, is the dentate nucleus. Though the dentate nucleus is missing in most mammals, it is largest in primates with the highest learning capabilities. A smaller area, the neodentate nucleus is present only in humans and may have a significant role in thinking. Neurologist Robert Dow of Portland, Oregon, was one of the first to make the links. One of his patients had cerebellar damage and—surprisingly—impaired cognitive function (S. Richardson 1996, p. 102). Suddenly, linking movement and thinking became inescapable.

Just how important is movement to learning? Ask neurophysiologist Carla Hannaford and she'll spend all day telling you. She says the vestibular (inner ear) and cerebellar system (motor activity) is the first sensory system to mature. In this system, the inner ear's semicircular canals and the vestibular nuclei are an information gathering and feedback source for movements. Those impulses travel through nerve tracts back and forth from the cerebellum to the rest of the brain, including the visual system and the sensory cortex. The vestibular nuclei are closely modulated by the cerebellum and also activate the reticular activating system (RAS), near the top of the brain stem. This area is critical to our attentional system, since it regulates incoming sensory data. This interaction helps us keep our balance, turn thinking into actions, and coordinate moves. That's why there's value in playground games that stimulate inner ear motion like swinging, rolling, and jumping.

Peter Strick at the Veteran Affairs Medical Center of Syracuse, New York, made another link. His staff has traced a pathway from the cerebellum back to parts of the brain involved in memory, attention, and spatial perception. Amazingly, the part of the brain that processes movement is the same part of the brain that's processing learning.

Here's another example. Neuroscientist Eric Courchesne of the University of California at San Diego says autism may be related to cerebellar deficits (L. Richardson 1996). His brain-imaging studies have shown that autistic children have smaller cerebellums and fewer cerebellar neurons. He also has linked cerebellar deficits with impaired ability to shift attention quickly from one task to another. He says the cerebellum filters and integrates floods of incoming data in sophisticated ways that allow for complex decision making. Once again, the part of the brain known to control movement is involved in learning. Surprisingly, there is no single "movement center" in our brain (Greenfield 1995). Movement and learning have constant interplay.

In Philadelphia, Glen Doman has had spectacular success with autistic and brain-damaged chil-dren by using intense sensory integration therapy. Over the years, many teachers who integrated productive "play" into their curriculum found that learning came easier to students.

At the 1995 Annual Society of Neuroscience Conference, W.T. Thatch Jr. chaired one of the most well-attended symposiums: "What Is the Specific Role of the Cerebellum in Cognition?" He's a researcher at the Washington University School of Medicine who's been pulling together data for years. The 800 attendees listened carefully as the panel made a collective assault on a neuroscience community blinded by years of prejudice. Nearly 80 studies were mentioned that suggest strong links between the cerebellum and memory, spatial perception, language, attention, emotion, nonverbal cues, and even decision making. These findings strongly implicate the value of physical education, movement, and games in boosting cognition.

Motor Development and Learning

There is, in fact, substantial biological, clinical, and classroom research that supports this conclusion. The area known as the anterior cingulate is particularly active when novel movements or new combinations are initiated. This particular area seems to tie some movements to learning. Prescott's early studies (1977) indicate that if our movements are impaired, the cerebellum and its connections to other areas of the brain are compromised. He says the cerebellum also is involved in "complex emotional behavior" (emotional intelligence). His rat experiments bear out his conclusions. Rats with cerebellar deficits did worse on maze testing.

Our brain creates movements by sending a deluge of nerve impulses to either the muscles or the larynx. Because each muscle has to get the message at a slightly different time, it's a bit like a well-timed explosion created by a special effects team. This amazing brain-body sequence is often referred to as a spatiotemporal (space-time) pattern. Researcher William Calvin calls it a cerebral code. While simple movements like gum chewing are controlled by basic brain circuits nearest the spinal cord, complex movement—like dance steps, throwing a ball, or doing a science experiment—is quite different. Some simple movements, like those with sequences, are controlled at the subcortical levels, like the basil ganglia and cerebellum. But novel movements shift focus in the brain because it has no memories to rely on for execution. Suddenly we engage the prefrontal cortex and the rear two-thirds of the frontal lobes, particularly the dorsolateral frontal lobes. This is an area of the brain often used for problem solving, planning, and sequencing new things to learn and do (Calvin 1996).

Many researchers (Houston 1982, Ayers 1972, Hannaford 1995) verify that sensory motor integration is fundamental to school readiness. In a study done in Seattle, Washington, 3rd grade students studied language arts concepts through dance activities. Although the districtwide reading scores showed a decrease of 2 percent, the students involved in the dance activities boosted their reading scores by 13 percent in 6 months (Gilbert 1977). A complete routine included spinning, crawling, rolling, rocking, tumbling, pointing, and matching. Lyelle Palmer of Winona State University has documented significant gains in attention and reading from these stimulating activities (Palmer 1980). While many educators know of this connection, nearly as many dismiss the connection once children pass 1st or 2nd grade. Research sug-

gests the relationship between movement and learning continues throughout life. The drama class at Garfield High School in Los Angeles gives students new hope for life skills success. The sensory-motor skills learned as children, through both play and orchestrated school activities, mean the proper neural pathways have been laid (Miller and Melamed 1989).

How critical is early movement? There may be a link between violence and lack of movement. Infants deprived of stimulation from touch and physical activities may not develop the movement-pleasure link in the brain. Fewer connections are made between the cerebellum and the brain's pleasure centers. Such a child may grow up unable to experience pleasure through usual channels of pleasurable activity. As a result, the need for intense states, one of which is violence, may develop (Kotulak 1996). With sufficient supply of the needed "drug" of movement, the child is fine. Deprive him or her of it, and you get problems.

Physical Education and Learning

An astonishingly high 64 percent of K–12 American students do not participate in a daily physical education program (Brink 1995). In William Greenough's experiments at the University of Illinois, rats who exercised in enriched environments had a greater number of connections among neurons than those who didn't. They also had more capillaries around the brain's neurons than the sedentary rats (Greenough and Anderson 1991). In the same way that exercise shapes up the muscles, heart, lungs, and bones, it also strengthens the basal ganglia, cerebellum, and corpus callosum, all key areas of the brain. We know exercise fuels the brain with oxygen, but it also feeds it neurotropins (high-nutrient food) to enhance growth and greater connections between neurons. Aerobic conditioning also has been known to assist in memory (Brink 1995). Figure 9.2 illustrates the key pathways between movement and learning.

Researchers James Pollatschek and Frank Hagen say, "Children engaged in daily physical education show superior motor fitness, academic performance and attitude toward school as compared to their counterparts who do not participate in daily physical education" (1996, p. 2). Aerobic and other forms of "toughening exercises" can have enduring mental benefits. The secret is that

physical exercise alone appears to train a quick adrenaline-noradrenaline response and rapid recovery. In other words, by working out your body, you'll better prepare your brain to respond to challenges rapidly. Moderate amounts of exercise, 3 times a week, 20 minutes a day, can have very beneficial effects.

Neuroscientists at the University of California at Irvine discovered that exercise triggers the release of BDNF, a brain-derived neurotrophic factor (Kinoshita 1997). This natural substance enhances cognition by boosting the ability of neurons to communicate with one another. At Scripps College in Claremont, California, 124 subjects were divided equally into exercisers and nonexercisers. Those who exercised 75 minutes a week demonstrated quicker reactions, thought better, and remembered more (Michaud and Wild 1991). Because studies suggest that exercise can reduce stress, there's a fringe benefit too. Chronic stress releases the chemicals that kill neurons in the critical area of the brain for long-term memory formation, the hippocampus. Brink (1995) says that physical exercise is still one of the best ways to stimulate the brain and learning (Kempermann, Kuhn, and Gage 1997).

There's other evidence for the potency of physical movement. We know that much of the brain is involved in complex movements and physical exercise—it's not just "muscle work." In fact, depending on the type of workout, the part of the brain involved in almost all learning, the cerebellum, is in high gear (Middleton and Strick 1994). In a Canadian study with more than 500 schoolchildren, those who spent an extra hour each day in a gym class far outperformed at exam time those who didn't exercise (Hannaford 1995). Dustman's research (Michaud and Wild 1991) revealed that

---

FIGURE 9.2

Neural Relationships Between Movement and Learning

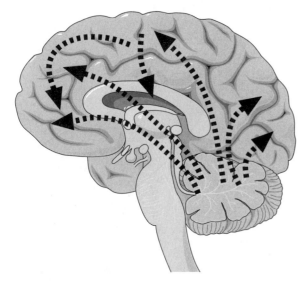

Projections of axons are far greater *from* areas associated with the storage and production of movement *to* areas of cognition than the reverse. This suggests that movement may influence cognition more than earlier believed.

among three test groups, the one that had the vigorous aerobic exercise improved short-term memory, reaction time, and creativity. All K–12 students need 30 minutes a day of physical movement to stimulate the brain, says the President's Council on Fitness and Sports. The Vanves and Blanshard projects in Canada revealed something even more dramatic. When physical education time was increased to one-third of the school day, academic scores went up (Martens 1982).

The Movement Arts

Three countries near the top in rankings of math and science scores (Japan, Hungary, and Netherlands) all have intensive music and art training built into their elementary curriculums. In Japan, every child is required to play a musical instrument or be involved in choir, sculpture, and design. Teaching students art also has been linked to better visual thinking, problem solving, language, and creativity (Simmons 1995). Many studies suggest that students will boost academic learning from games and so-called "play" activities (Silverman 1993). The case for doing something physical every day is growing. Jenny Seham of the National Dance Institute (NDI) in New York City says she has observed for years the measurable and heartwarming academic and social results of schoolchildren who study dance. Seham bubbles with enthusiasm over positive changes in self-discipline, grades, and sense of purpose in life that her students demonstrate. She's now in the process of quantifying the results of over 1,500 kids who dance weekly at NDI.

Researchers know certain movements stimulate the inner ear. That helps physical balance, motor coordination, and stabilization of images on the retina. David Clarke at Ohio State University's College of Medicine has confirmed the positive results of a particular type of activity—spinning (1980). With merry-go-rounds and swings disappearing from parks and playgrounds as fast as liability costs go up, there's a new worry: more learning disabilities. Clarke's studies suggest that certain spinning activities led to alertness, attention, and relaxation in the classroom. Students who tip back on two legs of their chairs in class often are stimulating their brain with a rocking, vestibular-activating motion. While it's an unsafe activity, it happens to be good for the brain. We ought to give students activities that let them move safely more often like role plays, skits, stretching, or even games like musical chairs.

Give a school daily dance, music, drama, and visual art instruction in which there is considerable movement, and you might get a miracle. In Aiken, South Carolina, Redcliffe Elementary test scores were among the lowest 25 percent in the district. After a strong arts curriculum was added, the school soared to the top 5 percent in 6 years (enough for the students to progress from 1st through 6th grade). This Title I rural school with a 42 percent minority student base showed that a strong arts curriculum is at the creative core of academic excellence—not more discipline, higher standards, or the three Rs (Kearney 1996).

Arthur Stone of the State University of New York at Stony Brook says having fun may be good for your health. It decreases stress and improves the functioning of the immune system for three days after the fun. Most kids enjoy dance, arts, and games. It's not just good for the brain, it feels good, too. Through primate experiments, neurophysiologists James Prescott and Robert Heath found that there's a direct link from the cerebellum to the pleasure centers in the emotional system (Hooper and Teresi 1986). Kids who enjoy playground games do so for a good reason: Sensory-motor experiences feed directly into their brains' pleasure centers. This is not of trivial importance; enjoying school keeps students coming back year after year.

Practical Suggestions

Today's brain, mind, and body research establishes significant links between movement and learning. Educators ought to be purposeful about integrating movement activities into everyday learning. This includes much more than hands-on activities. It means daily stretching, walks, dance, theater, drama, seat-changing, energizers, and physical education. The whole notion of using only logical thinking in a mathematics class flies in the face of current brain research. Brain-compatible learning means that educators should weave math, movement, geography, social skills, role play, science, and physical education together. In fact, Larry Abraham in the Department of Kinesiology at the University of Texas at Austin says, "Classroom teachers should have kids move for the same reason that P.E. teachers have had kids count" (1997). Physical education, movement, drama, and the arts can all be one continual theme. Don't wait for a special event. Here are examples of easy-to-use strategies.

Goal Setting on the Move

Start class with an activity where everyone pairs up. Students can charade or mime their goals to a partner or go for a short walk while setting goals. Ask them to answer three focusing questions such as

- What are my goals for today and this year?
- What do I need to do today and this week in this class to reach my goals?
- Why is it important for me to reach my goals today?

You can invent any questions you want or ask students to create some, too.

Drama, Theater, and Role Plays

Get your class used to daily or at least weekly role plays. Have students do charades to review main ideas. Students can organize extemporaneous pantomime to dramatize a key point. Do one-minute commercials adapted from television to advertise upcoming content or review past content.

Energizers

Use the body to measure things around the room and report the results. For example, "This cabinet is 99 knuckles long." Play a Simon-Says game with content built into the game: "Simon says point to the South. Simon says point to five different sources of information in this room." Do team jigsaw processes with huge, poster-sized mind-maps. Get up and touch, around the room, seven colors in order on seven different objects. Teach a move-around system using memory cue words. For example, "Stand in the room where we first learned about. . . ."

Ball toss games can be used for review, vocabulary building, storytelling, or self-disclosure. Students can rewrite lyrics to familiar songs in pairs or on a team. The new words to the song are a content review; then they perform the song with choreography.

Get physical in other ways, too. Play a tug-of-war game where everyone chooses a partner and a topic from a list that all have been learning. Each person forms an opinion about the topic. The goal is for each student to convince a partner in 30 seconds why his or her topic is more important. After the *verbal* debate, the pairs form two teams for a giant tug of war for a *physical* challenge. All partners are on opposite sides.

Cross-Laterals

Learn and use arm and leg crossover activities that can force both brain hemispheres to "talk" to each other better. "Pat your head and rub your belly" is an example of a crossover. Other examples include marching in place while patting opposite knees, patting yourself on the opposite shoulder, and touching opposite elbows or heels. Several books highlight these activities, including *Brain Gym* by Paul Dennison and *Smart Moves* and *The Dominance Factor* by Carla Hannaford.

Stretching

To open class, or anytime that you need some more oxygen, get everyone up to do some slow stretching. Ask students to lead the group as a whole or let teams do their own stretching. Allow learners more mobility in the classroom during specific times. Offer them errands, make a jump rope available, or simply let them walk around the back of the class as long as they do not disturb other students.

In general, you need to do all that you can to support physical education, the arts, and movement activities in your classroom. Make it a point to stand up for these activities in your school and district, too.

We are in a time when many children don't participate in physical education. Budget cuts often target the arts and physical education as "frills." That's a shame because there's good evidence that these activities make school interesting to many students *and* they can help boost academic performance. "Physical activity is essential in promoting normal growth of mental function," says Donald Kirkendall (Pollatschek and Hagen 1996, p. 2). Carla Hannaford says, "Arts and athletics are not frills. They constitute powerful ways of thinking, and skilled ways of communicating with the world. They deserve a greater, not lessor portion of school time and budgets" (1995, p. 88).

While it's counterproductive to make it more important than school itself, movement must become as honorable and important as so-called "book work." We need to better allocate our resources in ways that harness the hidden power of movement, activities, and sports. Norman Weinberger, a scientist in the Department of the Neurobiology of Learning and Memory at the University of California at Irvine, says, "Arts education facilitates language development, enhances creativity, boosts reading readiness, helps social development, general intellectual achievement, and fosters positive attitudes towards school" (1995, p. 6). This attitude has become more and more prevalent among scientists who study the brain. It's time for educators to catch on.

10 The Brain as a Meaning-Maker

When students say, "School is boring," part of the comment reflects a common adolescent feeling. Yet there's more to it: Learners want school to be worthwhile and meaningful. With so many different personalities, cultures, and types of students, how can school be meaningful for everyone? The theme of this chapter is that you can make learning richer and more appealing by purposely arranging the conditions for greater meaning.

The Search for Meaning

Traditionally, schools were a social arena and a delivery system for information. There wasn't much thought about whether the information was meaningful or not. The Information Age changed all that. While a 1950s learner was exposed to a few textbooks, three network television channels, some novels, and several magazines, today it's very different. The sheer volume of accessible information makes us recoil. Hundreds of television channels and multitudes of magazines and books are readily available. There are thousands of Web sites, countless Internet contacts, e-mail, faxes, cell phones, and pagers to assault the brain's information processing system.

While the brain is quite adept at learning, the amount of information criss-crossing our lives today may be a hundred- or thousand-fold compared to what it was just 50 years ago. This virtual avalanche of data can cause us to simply "shut off" as a coping mechanism. In schools, more classes, more content, and more information to learn can have a negative effect on students: stress from information overload. One of the solutions is to ensure the *quality* of information, not the *quantity*. We can do that by purposely orchestrating meaning. A delightful fringe benefit is that the exploration for meaning can be very intrinsically motivating.

Researchers tell us there are two types of meaning: reference and sense meaning (Kosslyn 1992, p. 228). Others refer to meaning as "surface" or "deeply felt" (Caine and Caine 1994). The first is a sort of pointer meaning, a dictionary definition that refers to the lexical territory of the word. For example, raincoat is an "oversized waterproof cloth or plastic garment." But the "sense" meaning of the word is different. While I know what a raincoat is, it means little to me personally. I live in a climate where it rarely rains (San Diego). The raincoat I own is used only rarely (when I travel) and seems like a waste of closet space most of the time.

Contrast this to a very different "sense" or a "deeply felt" meaning. Let's say you wear your raincoat 50–60 days a year because you live in an area where it rains often. Your raincoat may protect you from rain, be a good-looking addition to your wardrobe, and get you compliments. Your raincoat has "meaning sense" to you, with years of memories. It's more than a garment; it's both a necessity and a "friend."

In the classroom, the concept of the Vietnam War can be presented at the surface level or with deeply felt meaning. The latter might happen if the teacher is a Vietnam veteran who shares experiences with his or her students. In this chapter, we'll avoid the dictionary type of "pointer" meaning and deal with the "sense" type of meaning.

The Biology of Meaning

Many of our deeply felt meanings in life are built in, sort of hard wired into our brains. An example would be the human response of sadness to sickness and death. Humans have simply learned, over the centuries, to value life over death. One suspect for this mechanism is that the release of emotion-based chemicals can actually change the physical structure of the brain. Research by Nobel laureate Roger Sperry (Thompson 1993) indicates that chemical gradients in rats stimulate the growth and direction of axons toward a particular target cell. The changed organism may have an adaptive advantage over one who has not developed this response. For example, the fear of a quickly approaching large predator is automatic. In ancient times, humans who responded to this appropriate fear probably had a much greater survival rate.

Meaning that is not hard wired is a bit trickier. This "constructed" meaning might be more like a satisfying Thanksgiving holiday with family or a student's challenging science project. PET scans reveal the experience of meaning has a biological correlate, but it depends on what type of meaning. When something is meaningful during reading, there's usually more activity (as measured by glucose consumption) in the left frontal, temporal, or parietal lobe, says University of Oregon's Michael

FIGURE 10.1

Meaning-Making Occurs in Many Areas of the Brain

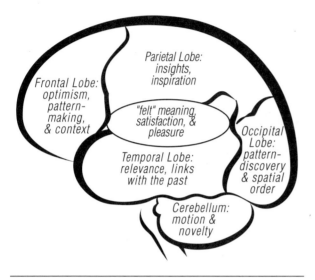

Posner. If it's a more spiritual meaning, it's probably a parietal lobe activity, says V.I. Ramachandran at the University of California at San Diego. If it's an emotionally felt meaning, it may show activity in the frontal, occipital, and mid-brain areas, says University of Iowa's Antonio Damasio. If it's an "Ah-ha!" type of meaning, it is more likely a left frontal lobe activity. These diverse areas of location suggest that the concept of meaning also may be diverse (see fig. 10.1).

In short, meaning is complex. We know the correlations, but we don't have causal relationships. Evidence suggests these factors are likely: relevance, emotions, and context and pattern making. Relevance is a function of the brain's making a connection from existing neural sites. Emotions are triggered by the brain's chemistry, and context triggers pattern making that may be related to the formation or activation of larger neural fields. All meaning has at least one of those three ingredients,

but the reverse is not true. Something could be relevant and still be meaningless at the same time. Eating a nutritionally sound diet is very relevant. It might also have little meaning to most students.

The Importance of Relevance

What's the biology of relevance? It's one of the easiest, most commonly made, types of meaning. It happens on a simple cellular level. An already existing neuron simply "connects" with a nearby neuron. If the content is irrelevant, it's unlikely a connection will be made. While neurons are constantly firing, much of the time it's an inaudible chatter. Relevant connections are made more often, and that strengthens them. Every thought you think increases the chances of your thinking that thought again.

Some thoughts activate entire neural fields that may cross cell and axon boundaries. The greater the number of links and associations that your brain creates, the more neural territories involved and the more firmly the information is woven in neurologically. Conversations were so rich with Nobel laureate Buckminster Fuller because he could make so many associations that nearly everything reminded him of nearly everything else. A conversation about birds might bring in the history of bird watching, the changing food supply, economics of conservation, geography, the economics of birds, biology, love, rituals, myth, politics, and beauty. To him, nearly everything was relevant. For many students, the problem is the opposite. Classroom information lacks the personal relevance necessary for any meaning.

Practical Suggestions for Making Meaning

Never assume that because something is relevant to you, it's relevant to your students. Help them discover relevance, but don't impose your connections. Give students time to link prior learning with discussion, mapping, and journaling. Use the power of current events, family history, stories, myth, legends, and metaphors to help make the learning relevant. Throughout human history, stories have been fundamental to understanding and valuing the people and lessons of the past. Let learners explain what is taught in their own words. You can use relevant personal stories. You might also tie in the local or national media. Encourage students to share their own experiences.

Teachers who continue to emphasize one-sided lecture methods are violating an important principle of our brain: Essentially we are social beings and our brains grow in a social environment. Because we often forge meaning through socializing, the whole role of student-to-student discussion is vastly underused. When used properly, cooperative learning is highly brain compatible. Talking, sharing, and discussing are critical; we are biologically wired for language and communicating with one another. Use discussion questions or let students pair up and share personal experiences. Allow time for "free association." You might ask questions like "Have you ever had this happen?" Or, "Could you compare and contrast this to a personal experience?"

The Importance of Emotions

Why and how do emotions engage meaning? Neurobiologist James McGaugh at the University of California at Irvine says that intense emotions trigger the release of the chemicals adrenaline, norepinephrine, and vasopressin. He adds, "[T]hey signal the brain, 'This is important—keep this!' " (Hooper and Teresi 1986). There's little doubt about it: Emo-

tions and meaning are linked. The question often asked is, "Which comes first, the emotion or the meaning?" It's a bit like the chicken-and-egg question. The systems are so interconnected that chemicals of emotion are released virtually simultaneously with cognition (Hobson 1994, LeDoux 1996).

We generate some emotion about what is happening on a moment-by-moment basis. However, most of our emotional states are not very intense. In general, we experience emotion only in regard to that which matters, say psychologists Bernice Lazarus and Richard Lazarus. We know that our sense of evaluation of events, people, and things seems to give things meaning ("Is it good or evil?"). We have been taught that the ability to discriminate between good and bad is a cognitive function, based on life experience. That's only partially true. When we evaluate, we are imbuing feelings to the content. This suggests the link between feelings and meaning. It's all processed at an unconscious level in the middle of the brain and brain stem area (Cytowic 1993 and LeDoux 1996).

Lazarus and Lazarus add, "[T]he dramatic plot or personal meaning that defines each emotion is universal in the human species. . . . [R]egardless of culture, no competent person fails to understand strong emotional events. . . ." (Lazarus and Lazarus 1995). Emotions engage meaning and predict future learning because they involve our goals, beliefs, biases, and expectancies. You can tap into this process. When your students do goal setting, it is their emotions that create the goal and their vested interest in achieving the goal. To invoke these emotions, have students share with another person why they want to reach their goals.

In a classroom, emotional states are an important condition around which educators must orchestrate learning. Students may be bored with the lesson, afraid of an upcoming test, or despondent about a drive-by shooting. They might be hyper about an upcoming sporting event, the preceding physical education class, or a relationship. Instead of trying to eliminate the emotions so we can get to the "serious cognitive" learning, it makes more sense to integrate them into our curriculum. Renate Caine, professor at California State University, San Bernadino, says that when we ignore the emotional components of any subject we teach, we deprive students of meaningfulness (Caine and Caine 1994). Emotions drive the threesome of attention, meaning, and memory. The things that we orchestrate to engage emotions in a productive way will do "triple duty" to capture all three.

Purposely Engaging Emotions

There's a big difference between simply evoking emotions randomly and productively inviting or purposely engaging emotions. In the first case, it's cheap and disrespectful. In the latter case, it's smart teaching. How can you help students develop more "deeply felt meaning" by engaging productive emotions? Here are some specific strategies.

Expression

Make sure the learner has a positive, safe way to express any negative or positive emotions. To start fresh, you might put a "dumping box" near the door so learners can toss in any negative feelings, either on paper or symbolically. Use a mind-calming visualization or relaxation exercise, or do something physical, such as a walk, cross-crawl, stretching, or games. Encourage dialogue time with partners or a small group, or sharing with the whole group. Give internal reflective time for journal writing, self-assessment, or goal setting.

Movement

Ensure that the learning engages positive emotions through role-play, theater, drama, mime, art, and simulations. Also use music, playing instruments, singing, cheers, shouting, debates, personal stories, improvisation, dance, quiz-show games, exercises, stretching, play, field trips, and student or guest speakers.

Stakes

Put higher stakes in the learning through the setting of goals or the possibility of public presentations to evoke emotional investment. Make choice a key ingredient as well as fun. As long as the students have resources and peer support, most are quite willing to do big or public projects.

Novelty

In animal studies, novelty has been one of the most potent experimental conditions leading to a hormonal response (Levine and Coe 1989). Too much novelty, and you'll create distress. Too little, and you get boredom. Make novelty relevant, social, and fun. Create immersion environments where the room has been redesigned or decorated as a city, new place, or foreign country. Let students design the classroom as a rain forest, an airplane, a business, or other country.

Sharing

Develop greater peer collaboration, make projects cooperative. Use partners, long-standing teams, or temporary groups for specialized activities.

Apprenticeships

Encourage the use of more relationship-driven learning by providing apprenticeship relationships with experts. Multi-age classrooms, big-brother/ big-sister programs, and community-active adults are perfect examples of support systems.

Think Big

Do fewer, but more complex projects, especially lengthy multi-level projects, with sufficient time and resources. Students in a science class could plan a five-year trip to Mars. The project would involve skills in math, science, problem solving, research, economics, and social skills. Complex projects present more opportunities for curiosity, mystery, social interaction, frustration, excitement, challenge, fulfillment, and celebration than shorter, simpler ones.

The Importance of Context and Patterns

In his book *Pattern Thinking*, Andrew Coward (1990) says the brain forms quick hierarchies to extract or create patterns. The patterns give context to information that otherwise would be dismissed as meaningless. This desire to form some kind of meaningful pattern out of learning seems innate. Children create games that organize behaviors, and they will arrange objects into patterns rather than leave them random. Adults organize dishes, cars, tools, sewing articles, businesses, file cabinets, and book chapters.

Researchers believe this patterning may begin on a micro level. Individual neurons do not seem to exhibit learning, only groups of neurons. These networks or "clouds" of neurons seem to be able to recognize and respond to meaningful learning. In fact, scientists are currently testing models of perception and learning that may mimic the brain's visual system (Bruce and Green 1990). These "connectionist" models mirror neuronal groups and synapses. Although they caution us in calling it a biological match, early findings are encouraging.

Other areas of neurobiology suggest pattern making may be innate. In a classic experiment, infants were shown a series of drawings. Each illustration had exactly the same elements as a human face. But only one had them in a coherent, human face shape and form. The others had the eyes, nose, hair, and mouth scrambled. To determine the interest and value to an infant, careful recordings were made of which figures were preferred by "gaze time." The pattern of a human face in its correct form had much more meaning to infants, even those a few days old (Franz 1961). Infants as young as 10 months or less are drawn to, and can recognize, patterns quicker than non-patterns (Mehler and Dupoux 1994). On videotape, infants show puzzled looks when presented with scattered, "unpatterned" material. These studies suggest we are wired to pay attention to certain patterns.

In tests of visual perception, researchers have shown not only that we are "naturals" at learning pattern discrimination but at applying it to other models. One researcher says it's the making of familiar connections (relevance) and locating conforming neural networks (pattern making) that are critical to the formation of meaning (Freeman 1995). How important is the process of pattern making to the brain? Child development expert Jane Healy says, "I am increasingly convinced that patterns are the key to intelligence. Patterning information means really organizing and associating new information with previously developed mental hooks" (1994, p. 49). Using the pattern-detecting and pattern-making areas of the brain is critical to proper development. Healy adds, "Children who don't learn to search for meaning are often good 'technicians' in the 1st and 2nd grade because they can deal with isolated data, but when the demands for comprehension increase, they 'hit the wall.' They simply can't assemble it and make sense out of it. Those who can are often thought of as more intelligent" (p. 50).

The fact that the brain elicits patterns to make a meaningful context was originally used as the reasoning behind integrated thematic instruction (Kovalik 1994). Yet there is a significant difference between what constitutes a pattern to a novice and to an expert. While the brain is a consummate pattern maker, intellectual maturity enriches the process dramatically. PET scans indicate a novice chess player burns more glucose and uses the step-by-step sequential left side of the brain. A master chess player uses less glucose while engaging larger patterns from the right side of the brain. And clearly, a historian would more likely see a centuries-old pattern in human behavior than a 4th grader. As a result, teachers can see the themes, connections, and relevancies that a student cannot because the adult's prior accumulated knowledge ties it all together. For younger students, learning has simply got to be hands-on, experiential, and relevant for patterns to develop.

Complex thematic patterns emerge *after* the brain has gathered sufficient data with which to make a meaningful context. Patterns can be forged and constructed only when enough essential "base" information is already known. As a result, thematic curriculum may be more useful to older students than younger ones. That's because the 16-year-old already has the existing milestones of knowledge from which to create a pattern. Metaphorically, he or she already knows the fence-posts, so it's easier to build the fence. In short, the evidence that links the brain's natural quest for meaning to integrated thematic instruction is more anecdotal and interpretive than biological. Kovalik now says that a point of view, a principle to operate from, is far more useful than the use of a simple yearlong theme. Universal concepts and core organizing principles like interdependency can make much better sense to youngsters.

There's also a great deal of value in the interdisciplinary and cross-disciplinary models. They create much more relevance and context and, more important, help students understand the connections in learning. In the classroom, it's the ability to see ideas in relation to others as well as how individual facts become meaningful in a larger field of information. Help students see how economics relates to geography, how mathematics links to art and music, and how ecology links to science and politics. Through discussion, arts, or visual thinking, students can make important, meaningful patterns.

In summary, we know the ingredients, but not the recipe. The ability to make meaningful patterns and use context seems to be activating frontal lobes. The ability to engage relevance uses our past experiences, and that domain is our temporal lobes. Meaning-making from emotional activation is more likely originating in the mid-brain's reward circuit. Thalamus, amygdala, and even lower parietal areas are involved. Meaning-making is complex. Any one of the three ingredients can trigger it, but none is guaranteed. This suggests we ought to evoke all of them in our general practices (see fig. 10.2).

FIGURE 10.2

Contributing Factors to Meaning-Making

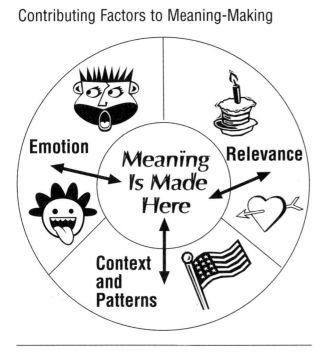

Practical Suggestions

Context can be either explicit or implicit. Implicit learning forms a powerful pattern called a mental model. Teachers who reveal their own mental models and elicit student models may be surprised at the value. These seem to be virtual "windows of the mind" that make explicit the implicit learning. Ask students *how* they know *what* they know through the use of "how" questions. How does democracy work? How does weather change? How does our body digest foods? How do you go about solving problems? These kinds of questions will draw out the patterns that can expose the boundaries, limitations, and genius in student thinking.

Explicit learning models can include graphic organizers. They are a way of giving information a base of context for better understanding and meaning. Studies indicate consistent success with this learning "by pattern" (Jones et al. 1988/1989). Mapping can serve as preexposure to the patterns of a topic. These web-like drawings are a graphic, creative visual display of the topic and the key relationships, symbols, and buzzwords that create meaning for the learner. Jeff King, director of staff development at the Art Institute of Dallas, says they help students learn more, recall more, and improve attitudes. Once made on paper, they can be shared with others to increase their meaning and to reinforce context and details.

The former Soviet Union had among the highest math and science achievement scores in the world. One insight into this achievement comes from the pioneering work of a legendary high school teacher, Victor Shatalov. As one of the country's most highly regarded teachers, Shatalov set high standards for success with his "nobody will fail" attitude. His students used graphic organizers with color coding to intensify important material. He also alternated daily between global and detail learning and shared his mental models for learning the material (Soloveichik 1979). There are many other ways to encourage more patterning for learners.

• Patiently answer the endless stream of "why" questions that children ask without sarcasm or being too brief or too wordy.

• Point out patterns in nature. For example, "Can you see all the leaf shapes in the trees?"

• Introduce skills of grouping objects, ideas, names, facts, and other key ideas.

• Simply read to kids and ask for patterns of organization. These might be cycles of cause and effect, problem and solution, or intense drama and down time.

• Ask questions that compare and contrast elements in nature.

• Help children learn to use jigsaw puzzles, blocks, and dominoes.

• Use stitchery to learn patterns. Sort buttons, needles, thread, and other sewing items. Use tool-boxes to sort nuts, bolts, screws, and tools. Use sorting skills for simple home, school, or life objects.

• Teach and learn sound patterns. Listen to the patterns in wildlife, such as bird calls.

• Before beginning a topic, give global overviews using overheads, videotapes or videodisks, and posters.

• Help students use motor skills to walk them through a learning process in advance of needing to know it.

• Days or weeks before actually starting a topic, prepare learners with oral previews, applicable games in texts or handouts, metaphorical descriptions, and mind-maps of the topic posted on the walls.

• When you finish with a topic, make sure that you allow learners to evaluate the pros and cons, discuss the relevance, and demonstrate their patterning with models, plays, and teachings.

More and more schools are realizing the importance of integrating educational practices with current brain theory. The kinds of practices illuminated in this book fit well with the current theory and practice of contextual learning and constructivism (Parnell 1996). Those who have advocated the purposeful and individual construction of meaning are right on the money. Ultimately, everyone has to make his or her own meaning out of things. It's not more content that students want; it's meaning. One of the things good schools do is understand the importance of meaning-making and provide the environment that includes the elements necessary for making meaning.

11 Memory and Recall

Memory and recall are critical elements in the learning process for very practical reasons. The only way we know that students have learned something is if they demonstrate recall of it. But why is it that just minutes or hours after learning something, many students seem to forget it? Why do they appear to experience a "faulty" memory? We adults often think we were better at remembering things in school than today's students are. It's true that schools rely less on rote memory for academic success than they did 50 years ago, but were we truly better at remembering when we were students?

This chapter considers memory and retrieval. By themselves, the latest discoveries about the brain may not be earth shaking. But taken as a whole, they provide a powerful framework for understanding and boosting memory and recall. There are some very good reasons for the near-universal phenomenon of forgetting things. Understanding this won't instantly give us all perfect recall, but it may illuminate some potential strategies for change. In fact, children today probably learn a great deal more than they demonstrate, and the ways we ask for recall are part of the problem of "forgetful students."

Key Memory Discoveries

Our outdated ideology about how the human memory works owes much to the misinterpretation of the important works of Canadian neurosurgeon Wilder Penfield. He reported that during surgery, an electrical stimulation of the temporal lobe produced episodes of recall, almost like seeing movie clips. Many drew the conclusion that our brains sort of "videotaped" life, and to remember things, our memories simply needed to be prompted. But, these episodes of recall occurred in only 3.5 percent of Penfield's patients. Some psychologists have since dismissed the supposed recall he reported as "prompted" (Fisher 1990), and the results have not been replicated by other surgeons.

Somehow, the erroneous but popular concept of a brain that records or videotapes life persisted. It's not that way at all. We can define the memory process as the creation of a persistent change in the brain by a transient stimulus. How does our brain do this? Researchers are still not 100 percent sure; it's been very frustrating to decipher the complete code to all of our memory processes. However, neuroscientists recently have made some important discoveries that may be helpful in the classroom.

Fluidity

Memory is a process, not a fixed thing or singular skill. There is no single location for all our memories. Certainly, many distinct locations of the brain are implicated with certain memories (see fig. 11.1). For example, memories of sound are stored in the auditory cortex. And researchers have found an area of the inner brain, the hippocampus, that becomes quite active for the formation of spatial and other explicit memories, such as memory for speaking, reading, and even recall *about* an emo-

tional event. Memories of names, nouns, and pronouns are traced to the temporal lobe. The amygdala is quite active for implicit, usually negative, emotional events (LeDoux 1996). Learned skills involve the basal ganglia structures. The cerebellum also is critical for associative memory formation, particularly when precise timing is involved as in the learning of motor skills. (Greenfield 1995). We also know that peptide molecules, which circulate throughout the body, also store and transfer information. This awareness helps us understand why "our body" seems to recall things at times.

Still, more of your "content knowledge" is distributed throughout the temporal lobes of the cortex. Today, scientists say it's better to think of memory as process rather than a specific location in the brain. The process for retrieval is much more consistent than is the location the memory was elicited from. Multiple memory locations and systems are responsible for our best learning and recall (Schacter 1992). This "spread the risk" strategy is why someone could lose 20 percent of the cortex and still be good at information retrieval. The different systems explain why a student can have a great recall for sports statistics and poor recall for famous people in history.

Formation

Scientists generally believe the specific process for formation of explicit memories is long-term potentiation (LTP). That's simply a rapid alteration in the strength of the synaptic connections. Susumu Tonegawa, a Nobel laureate at MIT, discovered that this process of LTP is mediated by genes that trigger a series of complex cascading steps (Saltus 1997). At the same time, neurobiologist Eric Kandel's team from Columbia University identified a

FIGURE 11.1

Locations of Our Stored Memories

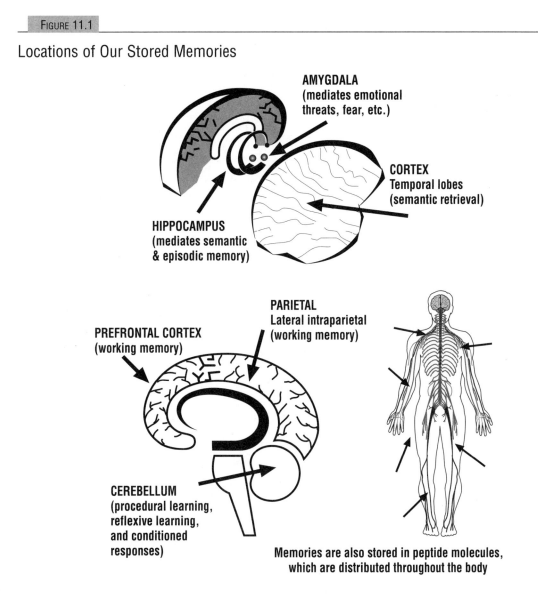

AMYGDALA
(mediates emotional
threats, fear, etc.)

CORTEX
Temporal lobes
(semantic retrieval)

HIPPOCAMPUS
(mediates semantic
& episodic memory)

PARIETAL
Lateral intraparietal
(working memory)

PREFRONTAL CORTEX
(working memory)

CEREBELLUM
(procedural learning,
reflexive learning,
and conditioned
responses)

Memories are also stored in peptide molecules,
which are distributed throughout the body

critical protein molecule, known as CREB. It serves as a logic switch, signaling nerve cells to store the memory as short-term or permanently engrave it in long-term memory (Wickelgren 1996). Tim Tully and Jerry Yin at Cold Spring Harbor Laboratory demonstrated that CREB activation gives fruit flies a photographic memory, or the ability to remember after just one trial what ordinarily required many trials (Lasley 1997). Most researchers believe the physical evidence of memory is stored as changes in neurons along specific pathways.

Randy Gallistel, Endel Tulving, William Calvin, and others emphasize that it's the retrieval *process* that activates dormant neurons to trigger our memories (Calvin 1996, Gazzaniga 1997). They argue that you cannot separate memory and retrieval: Memory is determined by what kind of retrieval process is activated. Each type of learning requires its own type of triggering. When enough of the right type of neurons firing in the right way are stimulated, you get a successful retrieval. In larger patterns, whole neuronal fields can be activated (Calvin 1996). For example, certain words, like "school," might activate hundreds of neuronal circuits, triggering a cerebral thunderstorm. The number one way to elicit or trigger recall is by association.

Chemical

Many modulatory compounds can enhance or depress recall if given at the time of learning. Examples of these are hormones, foods, or neurotransmitters. Calpain, which is derived from calcium, helps digest protein and unblock receptors. Researchers suspect that calcium deficiencies are linked to the memory loss of the elderly. Norepinephrine is a neurotransmitter that is linked to memories associated with stress. Phenylalanine, found in dairy products, helps manufacture norepinephrine, also involved in alertness and attention (Mark 1989).

Adrenaline acts as a memory fixative, locking up memories of exciting or traumatic events (Cahill, Prins, Weber, and McGaugh 1994). The brain uses the neurotransmitter acetylcholine in long-term memory formation. Increased levels of this neurotransmitter are linked to improved recall. Lecithin, found in eggs, salmon, and lean beef, is a dietary source that raises the choline levels and has boosted recall in many studies (Ostrander and Schroeder 1991). Choline is a key ingredient in the production of acetylcholine. Studies show that even the presence of household sugar in the bloodstream can enhance memory if given after a learning event (Thompson 1993).

Scientists postulate that the chemistry of our body, which regulates our physiological states, is a critical element in the subsequent triggering of our recall. Learning acquired under a particular state (happy, sad, stressed, or relaxed) is most easily recalled when the person is in that same state. This phenomenon of boosting recall by matching the learning and the test states even works with chocolate (Schab 1990). Eat chocolate during learning and you'll recall more at test time if you're eating chocolate once again. Realistically, however, this is only a small part of the whole equation.

Reconstruction

Our memories are not retrieved like chapter notes from a file cabinet. Most of them are reconstructed on the spot. There are two theories on how this miraculous process happens. One is that we have "indexes" that contain instructions for the brain on how to rekindle content; they don't index the content itself. University of Iowa researchers Hanna Damasio and Antonio Damasio call these "convergence zones," which help tie together the pieces so that you have appropriate retrieval. The best analogy is that your semantic memory works like "just in time" manufacturing, creating a "car on the spot" in its own auto parts store. This is an ingenious process since the "parts" are reusable on the next "car" or any other "car" you want to create.

For most of our word-based recalling, we use mental "indexes" to help us find the word we want (Damasio 1994). A word like *classroom* is very likely linked to several related indexes like school, work, kids, teacher, and meeting space. Our language is a classic example of having to pull hundreds of words "off the shelf" within seconds, to assemble even the most common sentences. This theory explains why a similar word—close, but still wrong—will come out of our mouths when we are trying to say something.

The other theory is that memories are frozen patterns waiting for a resonating signal to awaken them. They're like ripples on a bumpy road that make no sound until a car drives over them. Neurobiologist William Calvin says the content may be embedded in "spatiotemporal themes," which will resonate and create a critical mass needed for retrieval. Enough of that thought's identical copies have been made for the cerebral code to trip an "action switch" for you to recall (Calvin 1996). This computational theory explains why a student trying to remember information for a test comes up with the answer a half hour too late. It may take that long for the "intention to recall" to create enough "activated thought patterns" to hit critical mass. Earlier, the brain may have had too much other competing information processing to retrieve it.

Variety

Our separate memory pathways are used for different types of memories. Retrieval is quite specific. Neuroscientist Jeri Janowsky of Oregon Health Sciences University says it's common for us to be good at one type of recall, like faces and places, but not others, like addresses and dates. For example, consider the link-and-peg systems popularized by media memory experts like Harry Lorayne and Kevin Trudeau. These systems ask you to connect a new item with a previously memorized word or number. If the word *brain* was second on my list of things to recall, I might link it up to my second peg word, which happens to be the word *pants*. I'd visualize images of a brain spray painted all over my new pair of pants. The association is now pants = brain. Each additional word would have its own linking word. But can we all do these memory "tricks"? Most learners can use the peg systems and benefit greatly. Students who often are thought of as "lazy learners" may in fact simply be recalling only what they can. When your students can recall names and dates, it doesn't mean they'll be good at recalling the locations that geography requires. Figure 11.2 describes these memory pathways.

FIGURE 11.2

Memory Pathways

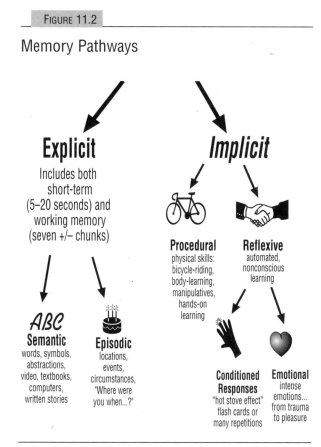

Retrieval

There is no firm distinction between how well a person thinks and how well he or she remembers (Turkington 1996). We can retrieve most everything we have paid attention to originally. But the success of that retrieval is highly dependant upon state, time, and context. To test this theory, researchers simulate the appropriate learning conditions, such as the right context or right state, then test for content. When done properly, the results are astonishing. Bahrick (1975, 1983, 1984) and Bahrick and Hall (1991) demonstrated remarkable recall for Spanish, mathematics, city streets, locations, name, and faces when careful attention was paid to context and state. For recognition tests, even elderly subjects who were given context stimulus scored 80 to 90 percent or more for classmate recognition after 35 years.

The variety of ways that we store and retrieve information tells us that we have to start thinking less of "our memory" and more of "which kind of memory and how it can be retrieved." School is a complex experience; by breaking apart all of the ways we learn, rehearse, and assess, we can uncover how to do a better job. By using the right system, in the right way, students can consistently experience better recall of their learning. This chapter considers all of the retrieval systems but focuses particularly on those that are most useful. The general process is outlined in fig. 11.3.

Explicit Memory

Neuroscientist Larry Squire of the University of California at San Diego says that the explicit or declarative memory system is formed in the hippocampus and stored in the medial temporal lobes.

At one time it was referred to as our conscious memory, but many researchers now say it's simply the one we can explain, write about, and describe (Schacter 1996). In general, it's the one that is used the most in schools when we ask for an exam-type recall or an essay. It comes in several forms including the more word-based semantic memory and the event-type episodic memory.

Semantic Pathways

Semantic memory is also known as explicit, factual, taxon, or linguistic memory. It's part of our declarative system and includes the names, facts, figures, and textbook information that seem to frustrate us the most. In fact, only explicit memory pathways have a short-term or a working memory.

Short-term refers to the length of time we can "hold it" in our head, which is usually 5–20 seconds. Working memory refers to the number of units of information we are holding. For the average adult, this is usually seven, plus or minus two. For example, we meet someone at a social gathering and forget the name mere seconds after an introduction. Or the mind goes blank after reading a single page of a book, and we recall nothing. Is there some reason we seem to forget so much?

In fact, there are several reasons. First, the storage of semantic memories seems to be distributed fairly well throughout the cerebrum. It's not that we are stupid or incapable; the brain may simply not be well-equipped to routinely retrieve this type of information. It requires the use of language triggers through association. This may be a relatively new need; humans have had little use for semantic recall until recent history when books, schools, literacy, and social mobility became common. This is, in fact, the weakest of our retrieval systems.

FIGURE 11.3

Key Steps in Memory Storage Processes

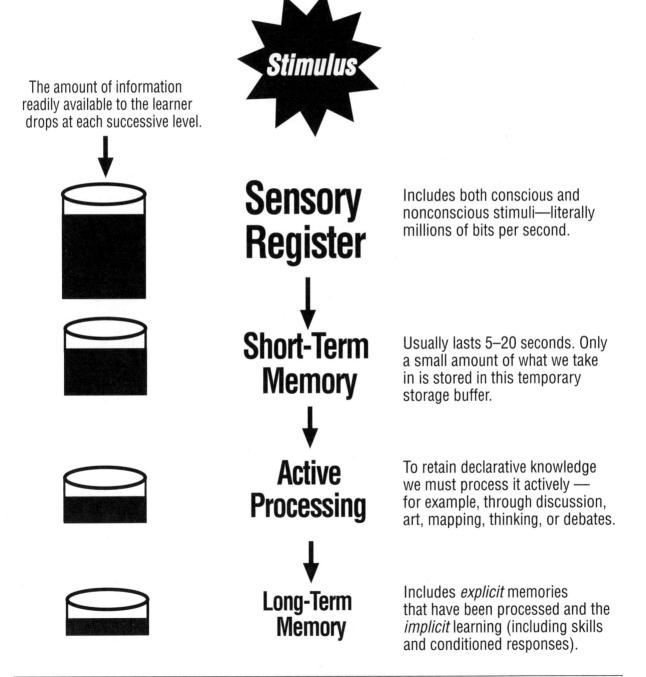

Stimulus

The amount of information readily available to the learner drops at each successive level.

Sensory Register

Includes both conscious and nonconscious stimuli—literally millions of bits per second.

Short-Term Memory

Usually lasts 5–20 seconds. Only a small amount of what we take in is stored in this temporary storage buffer.

Active Processing

To retain declarative knowledge we must process it actively — for example, through discussion, art, mapping, thinking, or debates.

Long-Term Memory

Includes *explicit* memories that have been processed and the *implicit* learning (including skills and conditioned responses).

In addition, much of our semantic learning is inaccessible because the original learning was trivial, too complex, lacked relevance or sufficient sensory stimulation, or was too "contaminated" with other learning. The largest portion of our learning is only temporarily extinct say Capaldi and Neath (1995). It can be recalled under the right conditions, as long as attention was paid initially. Their contention, which is shared by many, is that forgetfulness is merely a "temporary performance deficit." (Students will tell you that they often recall important items after the test is over, too late for any grade boost.)

Our semantic retrieval process is affected by "when" as much as by "what" is learned. Studies indicate small efficiency increases when we recall details and text learned in the morning and relationships in the afternoon (Oakhill 1988). Some researchers suggest the daily rise in levels of the neurotransmitter acetylcholine may contribute to this (Hobson 1994). We also seem to remember things that are new, first on a list, different from others, or just unique. If the novelty is strong enough, the likely recall of the material goes up dramatically.

Our semantic memory lives in the world of words; it's activated by association, similarities, or contrasts. The capacity limitations are more strongly influenced by the strength of associations made than the sheer quantity of items. We remember best in chunks, which are single thoughts, ideas, or groups of related ideas. For a 3-year-old, the normal limitation is about 1 chunk ("Put your shoes away, please"). For a 5-year-old, the limit is 2 chunks; for a 7-year-old, 3 chunks. This increases up to 7 chunks by age 15. Our "working" memory is limited by chunks and is usually good for less than 20 seconds unless rehearsed, reviewed, or reactivated.

Unfortunately, this type of memory requires strong intrinsic motivation. This is often described as textbook, handout, or "book learning." Teacher usage of this increases by ascending grade levels, and student frustration and failure increases accordingly each year. Teachers who require moderate to large amounts of recall from texts are, at best, developing self-discipline in the learners. At worst, they create discouraged learners who feel unnecessarily incompetent. Should we throw out traditional "book learning"? No, it's useful for many, many reasons. Students still need facts, directions, references, and safety information. They still need to read poetry, novels, letters, and texts. On the other hand, if you ask students what they have learned that was interesting in the last year, most of it won't be semantic. It may be another type of memory called *episodic*.

Episodic Pathways

This system is also known as the loci, spatial, event, or contextual recall process. It's a thematic map ("a place in space") of your daily experiences. In this case, learning and memory are prompted by the particular location or circumstance. The formation of this natural memory involves the hippocampus and medial temporal lobe. It's motivated by curiosity, novelty, and expectations. It's enhanced by intensified sensory input, such as sights, sounds, smells, taste, and touch.

Our episodic memory process has unlimited capacity, forms quickly, is easily updated, requires no practice, is effortless, and is used naturally by everyone. Ask the content question, "What did you have for dinner last night?" and most people immediately ask themselves first, "Where was I?" The *location* triggers the content. Common examples are "Where were you when . . . the moon landing, an earthquake, a flood, a bombing, an assassination, the Challenger disaster occurred—or when your first child was born?"

How does this process work? Surprisingly, our visual system has both "what" (content) and "where" (location) pathways (Kosslyn 1992). Many researchers believe this information is processed by the hippocampus in a visual fabric, or "weave of mental space." Unfortunately, not everyone agrees on how this system of spatial, configural, and relational cues works. Somehow, though, we possess a back-up memory system based on locational cues because every life experience has to be, in some way, contextually embedded. Thus, all learning is associated with corresponding sights, sounds, smells, locations, touch, and emotions. You can't not "be somewhere" when you learn. All learning provides contextual cues.

Aromas can be a strong clue, because our olfactory memory has minimal erosion. Odor molecules dissolve in the mucus lining of the roof of the nose. The smell receptors are stimulated and trigger nerve impulses that, unlike our other senses, bypass the sensory integration center, the thalamus. In that way, smell goes directly to the brain's frontal lobes and, more important, limbic system. The brain's system for these "automatic memories" like a particular perfume, a home-baked ham, or freshly baked cinnamon rolls seems magical. It may be because smells have a such a direct expressway to the brain. They are, in fact, only one synapse away!

Episodic processing does have a major drawback: contamination. That occurs when you have too many events or material embedded in the same location (like months of learning in the same seat in the same classroom in the same school). It's like a virus renaming all the files in your computer with the same filename—the information is there,

but it's nearly useless. This often happens to students who really do know their material but lack the specific "hooks" or mental "file names" to retrieve all their learning. It helps us understand why students like multiple-choice test formats; they provide the prompts that the brain needs. Forgetting occurs because such cues are rarely present when the recall is needed.

Implicit Memory

Neuroscientist Larry Squire found that he could have amnesic patients either succeed or fail on a task simply by changing the instructions. The patients had temporal lobe damage and were given lists of words to recall. If they were instructed to recall as many words as they could from an earlier list, they did poorly. But if they were told to simply say the first word that came to mind after a cue, their memory was as good as those without brain damage.

This led researchers to conclude that our ability to recall something depends on *which* pathway we access. Much information is still in our brain; it's not just a retrieval deficit. We know it, but don't *know* we know it. That's the implicit memory system. Skill learning, priming, and classical conditioning are all intact with temporal lobe damage, even if we can't answer simple questions about them (LeDoux 1996). That's because they involve other areas in the brain. The implication here is that students may know more than we think they do. We may have been using the wrong pathway for retrieval.

Procedural

This is often known as motor memory, body learning, or habit memory. It is expressed by student responses, actions, or behaviors. It's activated by physical movements, sports, dance, games, theater, and role play. Even if you haven't ridden a bike for years, you can usually do it again without practice. Procedural memory appears to have unlimited storage, requires minimal review, and needs little intrinsic motivation.

Memories of learned skills involve both the basal ganglia (located near the middle of the brain) and the cerebellum. In fact, the best examples of physical evidence found so far for *any* memory in the brain are those from skill memory. This evidence is located in the cerebellum (Thompson 1993). To the brain, the body is not a separate isolated entity. Body and brain are part of the same contiguous organism, and what happens to the body happens to the brain. This dual stimulus creates a more detailed "map" for the brain to use for storage and retrieval. (Squire 1992). Maybe that's why most students will tell you that the most memorable classroom experiences were based on hands-on learning.

This physical process (forming a line, role playing conflict resolution, doing a hands-on science experiment, cheerleading, or creating a project in an industrial arts class) is highly likely to be recalled. These are, in fact, the most commonly used methods for early childhood learning. A child's life is full of actions that require him or her to stand, ride, sit, try out, eat, move, play, build, or run. This creates a wider, more complex, and overall greater source of sensory input to the brain than mere cognitive activity. At school, this type of learning diminishes each year until it's virtually absent from all but a physical education, industrial or theater arts, or drama curriculum. Yet a summary of the research tells us that this learning is easier to master, is fairly well remembered, and creates lasting positive memories.

Reflexive

A great deal of what we recall is automatic. This memory pathway depends on a number of cortical pathways. They include the amygdala for emotional responses, muscle conditioning, and the cerebellum. Often referred to as "the hot stove effect," our reflexive retrieval system is full of instant associations. I say hot, you say cold; I say up, you say down; I say in, you say out. I reach my hand out to shake your hand, and your hand reaches out without a thought. In the classroom, a student drops something and tries to catch it. It's not unlike an orthopedic surgeon tapping on your knee to test the reflexes. In the classroom, reflexive retrieval can happen with flashcard repetition or other forms of "overlearning." That may be why a student who struggles with textbook learning can often excel with content-laden raps. The raps trigger the implicit memories of stored material and engage a different part of the brain than an essay would. Teachers would do well to include these with the many other types of retrieval methods mentioned.

Emotions get a privileged treatment in our brain's memory system. Several scientists at the Center for the Neurobiology of Learning and Memory at the University of California at Irvine have tested the effects of emotions on memory. Their studies (Cahill et al. 1994) suggest enhanced memory for events associated with emotional arousal. For many, unfamiliar and stressful events can trigger the release of chemicals such as adrenaline, cortisol, or ACTH. These serve as memory fixatives and strengthen the neural pathways. The negative emotions seem to be most easily recalled (LeDoux 1996), but all emotionally laden experiences are more easily recalled than neutral experiences. By working with patients with accidental damage to particular areas of the brain, it was discovered that intense experiences like fear, passion, and rage seem to be processed in the amygdala (Damasio 1994, LeDoux 1996).

Auditory memories are potent emotional triggers. A favorite song from your school days or the sounds from an emotionally charged football game may bring back earlier feelings. Researchers speculate that this stimulation takes separate pathways, distinct from the more mundane content-laden ones. This may be why traumatic events have such a lasting impact. They have their own "automatic" retrieval triggers. Students who get a standing ovation or a harsh rebuke from a teacher, or who enjoy and celebrate the completion of a project, are likely to recall that moment for years.

Practical Suggestions

Using the wrong retrieval process for the job usually leads to a performance deficit: "forgetting." By itself, that's not a disaster. But over time, it contributes to a lowered self-image and less of an effort. There are links between memory skills, better self-esteem, and school achievement. The good news is that it's fairly simple to make the changes necessary to promote these elements.

Explicit Declarative Strategies

The way to retrieve this type of learning is through strong activation with rhymes, visualization, mnemonics, peg words, music, and discussion. Otherwise, reading a chapter becomes an all-too-forgettable event. Remind students to stop often every quarter to half page and take notes, discuss what is read, or reflect. Conduct oral or written review, both daily and weekly. Students can pair up or rotate in teams to present daily reviews. You might repeat key ideas within 10 minutes of the original learning, then 48 hours later, and then tie it all in 7 days later. Spaced learning, with pauses and intervals for reflection, is valuable. Without the quiet processing time, much learning is never transferred to long-term memory.

To deal with the limitations of working memory, keep the chunks to a minimum. When giving directions and instructions to 6- to 9-year-olds, use small chunks, 1–3 items at a time. To older students, ages 10–17, use up to 7 chunks.

Morris and Cook (1978) assert it works to teach students how to use acrostics (first letter of each key word forms new word). The planets are: "My very excellent mother just sells nuts until Passover" (Mercury, Venus, Earth, Mars . . .). For years, we've learned the musical notes on the lines of the G-clef by memorizing "Every Good Boy Does Fine." We learn the Great Lakes by making one word of their first letters: HOMES (Huron, Ontario, Michigan, Erie, Superior).

To help students learn definitions, many teachers ask them to create action pictures that tie the two words together. To remember the word *semantic,* we could picture a "sea man, with ticks on his face" (se-man-tic) holding up a long list of words to memorize. That effectively unifies the two concepts in memory.

Many successful teachers find that mind-maps or other graphic organizers help students keep their learning fresh. Some teachers ask students to work with partners and a piece of flip-chart paper to create a weekly mind-map for review. The mind-map has a central organizing theme (like an author, a science topic, or a math concept). The outlying branches provide the detail.

We remember material best when it's structured and meaningful. Teachers might want to put the most important material first and last, so it's recalled better. Open and close the class with the three most important words or concepts for the day. Use music, props, or costumes to introduce them. Or, use openings for personal or controversial discussions that engage students emotionally. At the close, ask students to share what they have learned with their classmates.

In addition, wholes taught before parts are recalled better. Whether the subject is a Shakespearean play or an assignment in anatomy, our mind recalls best with context, a global understanding, and complete pictures to remember. You might introduce Shakespeare by showing a modern video first or making a pictorial overview map. Once students understand the relevance and overall themes, the details and deeper studying makes more sense. In anatomy, studying the whole body first will yield a better grasp of the parts.

Use poster-type peripherals to create more visually effective contexts. Have students draw out, organize, or symbolize key points on poster paper. Make sure they are easy to read, use illustrations, and feature strong colors. Put the overview up on the wall and leave it up weeks after the learning. Make and use storyboards (like oversized cartoon-like comic strip panels) of your key ideas. Better yet, ask students to make them.

Peer teaching and sharing works, too. Ask students to teach others what they've learned. They can pair up with others in different grade levels or with an adult. Create opportunities for students to discuss their learning, to debrief it and teach small chunks of it. Students can summarize in their own words what they have just learned. This is most effective when they are asked to analyze or break down their learning into smaller distinctions. Studies show (Matthews 1977) that it is the analysis of the material that aids in the recall of it.

What else do we know about recall? You remember most any learning that was temporarily interrupted. Cliffhangers do work! Introduce a pressing, relevant problem to solve, and leave brainstorming for solutions until the next day. We better recall material when we have reorganized it again and again. In a classroom, weather could be understood from the point of view of benefits or damage done, its geography, mythology, past meteorological history, or the impact of technology.

Attitude is important. Tell students, "Yes, you can." Start with a new attitude about memory and recall. Avoid saying, "Oops, I have to go back. I forgot something." A more accurate statement is, "Hey, I just *remembered* something; I've got to go back." In other words, you never forget anything; you just remembered it later than you wanted to!

Episodic Strategies

The movie *Dead Poets Society* showed examples of why students recalled so much of their learning. There were changes in location, circumstances, use of emotions, movement, and novel classroom positions. We know that learners remember much more when the learning is connected to a field trip, music, a disaster, a guest speaker, or a novel learning location. Follow up with a discussion, journal writing, a project, or peer teaching. Use location (context) changes. To enhance recall and better codify or "mark" the learning, learn concepts in different places so each location is a key clue to the content. Take the class outside for an introduction to something new.

Help students match learning and testing states. Studies tell us that the only matching states with low recall were neutral moods. Apparently learn-sad and test-sad or learn-happy and test-happy are far better than learn with no emotion, test with no emotion. The discrepancy between learning states and testing states is widely known among researchers as a source of performance loss (Bower 1981 and Overton 1984). There are two ways to affect this phenomenon. First, teach students how to better manage their own states at test time (for example, through relaxation methods or positive self-talk). Second, rehearse the learning in a variety of states to promote "recall resiliency." This strategy means that students can recall learning during a test because they've learned in a variety of states.

Many savvy teachers use reviews in a variety of states so that students can become acclimated to the range of emotions they'll likely feel at test time. That means use of timed quizzes, public quizzes, small group presentations, and structured practice taking timed mock tests. This will give students practice in many states, one of which may match the testing one. Remember to test in the same room in which students learned the material. This will better simulate the assessment conditions, and studies suggest students are more likely to test "up" to their learning levels.

Make stronger event-type memories by bringing in a guest speaker for special emphasis (maybe someone from your own school). Change where the class is taught from one side of the room to another. Create theme days (skeptical day, repeat day, brain day, opposite day) or theme weeks (fall, orange, sports) to add color to learning. On "skeptical day," students are asked to challenge their assumptions about nearly everything they know. During a theme week, there is one more set of "hooks" or associations for the students. For example, if the class is studying anatomy during "sports week," the extra connections of sports and the human body bring the topic to life. Real life studies of thematic classroom learning suggest it is common for the amount of learning to be doubled (Bower 1973).

Procedural Strategies

Nearly everything can be done with movement. If you have three points to make, ask students to rise. Ask them to take three steps in any direction. Introduce the first of the three points briefly as a preview. Include an action to help link it with the topic. Ask students to walk three more steps. Repeat this step. After you've introduced all three points, they have a seat. That's a simple example of body learning, as is the use of dance, sculpture, industrial arts, and total physical response for learning.

Embed emotions in the learning. Add a small daily celebration to heighten emotions. Because the first and last few minutes of a class will make the strongest impressions, invest more time on affecting emotions in the middle of class. Create role plays, improv theater, or reenactments. Have students make presentations to the class. Let them pair up or team up and debate what they've learned. Create or redo a song. Rewrite the lyrics of an old favorite, making a rap out of the key terms or ideas. Build a working model that embodies the key elements of the main ideas presented. Use dramatic concert readings: Read the key points you want to recall with dramatic instrumental music as a backdrop. Make up a story using the key items; it will supply a meaningful context for the items, and the plot provides an associative thread of ideas so that one triggers the next. The studies in this area are numerous; they include Bartlett and Santrock (1979) and Bower (1981).

Reflexive Strategies

The fill-in blank on a written test can be the prompt for semantic or reflexive retrieval, depending on how the material was learned and how much review was done. The more the practice, the more "automated" the learning, the more likely it will become reflexive. Flash cards, games like hopscotch, and other quick-reaction activities can help store and retrieve memories. The automatic nature of a rap means that it can also trigger implicit memories through both the physical motions and the auditory cues. Many students who would fail miserably with attempts at semantic storage and retrieval are real successes with the use of rap and other reflexive strategies.

Certainly, there's more to a better education than memory. Larger issues include questions such as, "How much should schooling require the need for memorization?" Or, "Is the teacher's role essentially content-driven (and leave it up to the students to figure out *how* to improve their recall) or catalytic (to empower students *how* to learn by teaching them these strategies)?" Although there's certainly less emphasis on the necessity to memorize volumes of material—except at the university levels in science, medicine, and law—it's still a critical skill. And as long as it remains critical, educators have an obligation to share the strategies described in this chapter with students.

Postscript

"So . . . What do I do on Monday?" As more and more educators are getting a taste of brain-compatible learning, many questions arise. Some of them can be answered by what we currently understand about the brain. We know enough now, for example, to help us design far better assessments, create more productive learning environments, and do a smarter job in staff development.

Other kinds of questions will have to wait for answers. For example, "What is the lasting impact of computers on the brain?" And, "At what age should children learn specific topics?" It's easy to speculate, but we're not quite sure about answers to those questions. Part of the reason we aren't sure is because very little of the current brain research is directed at education. It's driven by grants, pharmaceutical firms, and private funding. Each of them has its own agenda for what gets studied. It may be cancer, genes, cloning, drugs, or stress. As a result, educators have to take what applications of research are available.

As professionals, we must become engaged in systemic, action research. Does a certain type of music prime the brain for writing poems? Split your class and find out. Does lowering threat and stress encourage participation? Split your class into low and moderate stress, and try it out. We all want to be treated like professionals; let's start acting like curious, passionate learners who really want to know about the best ways for our students to learn.

Knowing critical information about how to do your job is no longer optional. May I suggest that understanding recent brain research and its connections to learning become standard requirements for educators? You don't need to be a biologist or neuroscientist to grasp these key concepts. Avoid getting hung up on the vocabulary or neural processes. In fact, too much interest in the biology of this movement may take up valuable time for something else more important: the practical work needed for the transformation of education.

This process has three steps. First, become more savvy about the brain. Learn the key ideas and principles. Second, use what you've learned at the pace you can do it best. And, third, go for the "big win" and begin school- and districtwide transformation. This information is not a fad or a staff development day to "do and get out of the way." It ought to be a long-term, guiding force in your everyday decision making: "Given what we understand about the brain and how it learns, is this idea good for student learning?"

Now, the real work begins. We must use what we know about the brain not just to stimulate our curiosity, but to actively engage educators in the change process. Use what we know about the brain, not just with students, but our staff, too. Brain-compatible specifics for staff development include dialogue time, choice, reflection, teams, journaling, peer coaching, more feedback, and experimentation. From those will come innovative

models that optimally develop each teacher's natural capacities. With minimal downside risk, we can create new, complex, orchestrated learning communities that have the capacity to push traditional achievement scores to new heights.

That, however, is not why I wrote this book. I'm more interested in how we can all build a better society. As an example, most families are still unfamiliar with what it takes in the first five years to get their child ready for school. That's why I suggest we start asking ourselves different questions. What kind of world might we have in 20 years? What might the citizens of tomorrow really need to know? Have we developed lifelong learners? Do students know about complex systems? Are we developing more participatory citizens for a democratic society? Are we developing better thinkers? Can they read, fill out forms? How can we better encourage more community service, art, music, and science? Do graduates have a love of learning anymore? The evidence suggests that collectively we are not successfully addressing those issues.

Is brain-compatible learning the answer? It's one of them. Fortunately, we do have enough insight already to make dramatic and powerful changes in how we conceptualize, design, and implement educational policy. While the research doesn't always give us the specific form or structure for *how* to shift the paradigm, it's clear that we have enough to figure it out. Don't wait for more or newer research—there will always be updates. It makes more sense to start with what you can do today and take the first step. Some follow-up resources are listed on page 126. Good luck. We are counting on you.

Glossary of Brain Terms

▶ **Acetylcholine.** A common *neurotransmitter*, particularly involved in long-term memory formation. Specifically released at neuromuscular junctions, it's present at higher levels during rest and sleep. These junctions are at the terminal between a motor nerve axon and a skeletal muscle fiber.

▶ **ACTH.** Also adrenocorticotropin hormone. This stress-related substance is produced by the pituitary gland. It's released into your system when you experience injury, emotion, pain, infections, or other trauma.

▶ **Adrenaline.** Under conditions of stress, fear, or excitement, this hormone is released from your adrenal gland into your bloodstream. When it reaches your liver, it stimulates the release of glucose for rapid energy. Abrupt increases caused by anger can constrict heart vessels, requiring the heart to pump with higher pressure. Also known as *epinephrine*.

▶ **Amygdala.** Located in the middle of the brain, this almond-shaped complex of related nuclei is a critical processor area for senses. Connected to the *hippocampus*, it plays a role in emotionally laden memories. It contains a huge number of opiate receptor sites implicated in rage, fear, and sexual feelings.

▶ **Axons.** These are the long fibers extending from the brain cells (*neurons*) that carry the output (an electrical nerve impulse) to other *neurons*. They can be up to a meter long. There is just one axon per *neuron*, but axons can subdivide to connect with many *dendrites*.

Axons often build up a fatty white insulation called *myelin*.

▶ **Basal ganglia.** Clusters of nuclei deep within the *cerebrum* and the upper parts of the brain stem that play an important part in producing smooth, continuous muscular actions in stopping and starting movement.

▶ **Brain stem.** Located at the top of the spinal cord, it links the *lower brain* with the middle of the brain and cerebral hemispheres. Often referred to as the *lower brain*.

▶ **Broca's area.** This is part of the left *frontal* area in the *cerebrum*. It converts thoughts into sounds (or written words) and sends the message to the motor area. Impulses go first to *Wernicke's area*, then to *Broca's area*.

▶ **Cerebellum.** A cauliflower-shaped structure located below the *occipital* area and next to the brain stem. The word is Latin for "little brain." Traditionally, research linked it to balance, posture, coordination, and muscle movements. Newer research has linked it to cognition, novelty, and emotions.

▶ **Cerebral cortex.** This is the newspaper-sized, 1/4-inch thick, outermost layer of the *cerebrum*. It's wrinkled, six layers deep, and packed with brain cells (*neurons*). *Cortex* is the Latin word for "bark" or "rind."

▶ **Cerebrum.** This is the largest part of the brain, composed of the left and right hemisphere. It has *frontal, parietal, temporal,* and *occipital lobes*.

▶ **Cingulate gyrus.** This structure lies directly above the *corpus callosum*. It mediates communication between the *cortex* and *mid-brain* structures.

▶ **Corpus callosum.** A white-matter bundle of 200–300 million nerve fibers that connect the left and right hemispheres. Located in the *mid-brain* area, it's about four inches long.

▶ **CORT.** Corticotropin is a steroid hormone released by the adrenal cortex during stress. It binds to a specialized neuronal receptor where regions in the amygdala and hippocampus are particularly impacted.

▶ **CRF.** Corticotropin release factor. A chemical secreted by the hypothalamus that prompts the pituitary gland to release a stress hormone, ACTH.

▶ **Dendrites.** These are the strand-like fibers emanating from the neuron. Similar to spider webs or cracks in a wall, they are the receptor sites for *axons*. Each cell usually has many, many *dendrites*.

▶ **Dentate nucleus.** A small structure in the *cerebellum*. Responsible for processing signals to other areas of the brain.

▶ **Dopamine.** A powerful and common *neurotransmitter*, primarily involved in producing positive moods or feelings. Secreted by *neurons* in the *substantia nigra, mid-brain,* and *hypothalamus*, it plays a role in movements, too. It's commonly in shortage in patients suffering from Parkinson's disease.

▶ **Endorphin.** A natural opiate, this *neurotransmitter* is similar to morphine. It is produced in the pituitary gland. Protects against excessive pain and is released with *ACTH* and *enkephalins* into the brain.

▶ **Enkephalin.** This morphine-like substance consists of five opiate-type amino acids. Released into the brain with *ACTH* and *endorphins* to combat pain.

▶ **Fornix.** A circular arrangement of fibers connecting the *hippocampus* to the *hypothalamus*.

▶ **Frontal lobes.** One of four main areas of the *cerebrum*, the upper brain area. Controls voluntary movement, verbal expression, problem solving, willpower, and planning. The other three areas of the *cerebrum* are the *occipital, parietal,* and *temporal*.

▶ **GABA.** Shorthand for gamma-aminobutyric acid. This common *neurotransmitter* acts as an inhibitory agent, an "off" switch. *Neurons* are constantly "chattering" with random firing, and GABA prevents the electrical impulse from moving down the *axon*.

▶ **Glial.** It is one of two major types of brain cells. The other is a *neuron. Glials* outnumber *neurons* 10-1 and also are known as interneurons. They carry nutrients, speed repair, and may form their own communication network. *Glial* is short for "neuroglia."

▶ **Glutamate.** An amino acid found in every cell in the body, it is also used in the nervous system as a "fast excitatory" neurotransmitter.

▶ **Hippocampus.** Found deep in the *temporal lobe*, central to the middle of the brain area. It is crescent shaped and strongly involved in learning and memory formation.

▶ **Hypothalamus.** Located in the bottom center of the middle of the brain area under the *thalamus.* Complex thermostat-like structure that influences and regulates appetite, hormone secretion, digestion, sexuality, circulation, emotions, and sleep.

▶ **Lateralization.** Refers to the activity of using one hemisphere more than another. The term "relative lateralization" is more accurate because we are usually using at least some of the left and right hemisphere at the same time.

▶ **Limbic system.** An older term coined by Paul MacLean in 1952. It describes a group of connected structures in the mid-brain area, which includes the *hypothalamus, amygdala, thalamus, fornix, hippocampus,* and *cingulate gyrus.*

▶ **Lower brain.** This is the lower portion of the brain composed of the *upper spinal cord, medulla, pons,* and some say the *reticular formation.* It sorts sensory information and regulates survival functions like breathing and heart rate.

▶ **Medulla oblongata.** Located in the *brain stem*, it channels information between the cerebral hemispheres and the spinal cord. It controls respiration, circulation, wakefulness, breathing, and heart rate.

▶ **Mid-brain.** Refers to the geographical area behind frontal lobes, above brain stem, and below parietal lobes. Structures within it include *thalamus, hippocampus,* and *amygdala.*

▶ **Myelin.** A fatty white shield that coats and insulates *axons.* They can help make the cells (*neurons*) more efficient and allow electrical impulses to travel up to 12 times faster. Habits may be a result of myelinated *axons.*

▶ **Neurotropin.** Any nutrient that enhances brain function. May include food, hormones, or medications.

▶ **Neuron.** One of two types of brain cells. We have about 100 billion of these. Receives stimulation from its branches, known as *dendrites.* Communicates to other neurons by firing a nerve impulse along an *axon.*

▶ **Neurotransmitters.** Our brain's biochemical messengers. We have more than 50 types of them. These usually act as the stimulus that excites a neighboring *neuron* or as an inhibitor to suppress activation of the electrical impulse traveling from the cell body down the *axon.*

▶ **NMDA (N-methyl-D-aspartate) receptor.** A receptor for the amino acid called *glutamate,* which is found in every cell in the body and which plays a central role in brain function.

▶ **Noradrenaline.** A common *neurotransmitter,* primarily involved in our arousal states: fight or flight, metabolic rate, blood pressure, emotions, and mood.

▶ **Occipital lobe.** Located in the rear of the *cerebrum.* One of the four major areas of the upper brain, this lobe processes our vision. The other three areas are *parietal, frontal,* and *temporal lobes.*

▶ **Oxytocin.** A peptide also know as the "commitment molecule." It's released during sex and pregnancy and influences "unlearning" and pair bonding.

▶ **Parietal lobe.** The top of our upper brain, it's one of four major areas of the *cerebrum.* This area deals with reception of sensory information from the body's opposite side. It also plays a part in reading, writing, language, and calculation. The other three lobes are the *occipital, temporal,* and *frontal.*

▶ **Peptides.** A class of hormones made of chains of amino acids. These proteins also serve as information messengers for states, moods, and thinking. They travel throughout the body.

▶ **Phoneme.** One of the smallest speech units, like the *m* of *mat* and *b* of *bat* that distinguish one word or utterance from another.

▶ **Pons.** Located near the top of the *brain stem*, above the *medulla*. It's a critical relay station for our sensory information.

▶ **Reticular formation.** A small structure, located at the top of the *brain stem* and bottom of *mid-brain* area. It's the regulator responsible for attention, arousal, sleep-awake, and consciousness.

▶ **Septum.** A thin partition or membrane between two body cavities or soft masses of tissues.

▶ **Serotonin.** A common *neurotransmitter*, most responsible for inducing relaxation and regulating mood and sleep. Antidepressants (like Prozac) usually suppress the absorption of serotonin, making it more active.

▶ **Substantia Nigra.** A group of darkly stained neurons in the *mid-brain* area that contains high levels of dopamine. These connect to the *basal ganglia* to control movement.

▶ **Synapse.** It's the junction communication point where *neurons* interact. When an axon of one *neuron* releases *neurotransmitters* to stimulate the *dendrites* of another cell, the resulting process where the reaction occurs is a *synapse*. The adult human has trillions of *synapses*.

▶ **Temporal lobes.** Located on the side of the *cerebrum* (in the middle of our upper brain, near our ears), it's an area believed responsible for hearing, senses, listening, language, learning, and memory storage. The other three major *cerebrum* areas are the *frontal*, *occipital*, and *parietal lobes*.

▶ **Thalamus.** Located deep within the middle of the brain, it is a key sensory relay station. It's also part of the body's reward system.

▶ **Vasopressin.** A stress-related hormone that is responsible partly for our aggression.

▶ **Vestibular.** The system found in the inner ear that helps maintain balance and judge a person's position in space, even with the eyes shut.

▶ **Wernicke's area.** Refers to the upper back edge of the *temporal lobe*. Here the brain converts thoughts into language.

Bibliography

Abraham, L. (February 28, 1997). Personal interview.

Ackerman, S. (1992). *Discovering the Brain.* Washington, D.C.: National Academy Press.

Ackerman, S. (1996). "Imaging the Field of Dreams." *BrainWork Newsletter* 6, 6: 7.

Altmaier, E.M., and D.A. Happ. (1985). "Coping Skills Training's Immunization Effects Against Learned Helplessness." *Journal of Social and Clinical Psychology* 3, 2: 181–189.

Amabile, T. (1989). *Growing Up Creative.* New York: Crown.

Armstrong, T. (1995). *The Myth of the ADD Child.* New York: Dutton/Penguin.

Atlas, J. (November 18, 1996). "The Fall of Fun." *New Yorker,* 68.

Ayers, J. (1972). *Sensory Integration and the Child.* Los Angeles: Western Psychological Services.

Ayers, J. (1991). *Sensory Integration and Learning Disorders.* Los Angeles: Western Psychological Services.

Bahrick, H.P. (1975). "Fifty Years of Memories for Names and Faces." *Journal of Experimental Psychology* 104: 54–75.

Bahrick, H.P. (1983). "The Cognitive Map of a City—Fifty Years of Learning and Memory." In *The Psychology of Learning and Motivation*, Vol. 17, edited by G.H. Bower, pp. 125–163. New York: Academic Press.

Bahrick, H.P. (1984). "Semantic Memory Content in Permastore: Fifty Years of Memory for Spanish Learned in School." *Journal of Experimental Psychology* 113: 1–29.

Bahrick, H.P., and L.K. Hall. (1991). "Lifetime Maintenance of High School Mathematics Content." *Journal of Experimental Psychology* 120: 20–33.

Bartlett, J.C., and J.W. Santrock. (1979). "Affect-Dependent Episodic Memory in Young Children." *Child Development* 50, 2: 513–518.

Begley, S. (February 19, 1996). "Your Child's Brain." *Newsweek,* 55–62.

Biederman, J., S. Faraone, S. Milberger, J. Guite, E. Mick, L. Chen, D. Mennin, A. Marrs, C. Ouellette, P. Moore, T. Spencer, D. Norman, T. Wilens, I. Kraus, and J. Perrin. (Winter 1996). "A Prospective 4-Year Follow-Up Study of Attention Deficit Hyperactive and Related Disorder." *Archives of General Psychiatry* 53, 5: 437–446.

Biederman, J., S. Milberger, S. Faraone, K. Kiely, J. Guite, E. Mick, S. Ablon, R. Warburton, and E. Reed. (June 1995). "Family-Environment Risk Factors for Attention-Deficit Hyperactivity Disorder: A Test of Rutter's Indicators of Adversity." *Archives of General Psychiatry* 52, 6: 464–470.

Black, J.E., B.J. Anderson, Li X Li, A.A. Alcantara, K.R. Isaacs, and W.T. Greenough. (May 1994). "Glial Hypertrophy Is Associated with Synaptogenesis Following Motor-Skill Learning, But Not with Angiogenesis Following Exercise." *Glia* 11, 1: 73–80.

Black, J.E., K.R. Isaacs, B.J. Anderson, A.A. Alcantara, and W.T. Greenough. (1990). "Learning Causes Synaptogenesis, While Motor Activity Causes Angiogenesis, in Cerebellar Cortex of Adult Rats." *Proceedings of the National Academy of Sciences* 87: 5568–5572.

Bliss, T.V.P., and T. Lomo. (1973)."Long Lasting Potentiation of Synaptic Transmission." *Journal of Physiology* 232: 331–356.

Bower, G.H. (October 7, 1973). "How to . . . uh . . . Remember!" *Psychology Today,* 63–70.

Bower, G.H. (February 1981). "Mood and Memory." *American Psychologist* 36, 2: 129–148.

Brink, S. (May 15, 1995). "Smart Moves." *U.S. News & World Report.* (Online database.)

Bruce, V., and P. Green. (1990). *Visual Perception.* East Sussex, U.K.: Lawrence Erlbaum and Associates.

Cahill, L., B. Prins, M. Weber, and J. McGaugh. (October 20, 1994). "Adrenergic Activation and Memory for Emotional Events." *Nature* 371, 6499: 702–704.

Caine, R.N., and G. Caine. (1994). *Making Connections: Teaching and the Human Brain.* Menlo Park, Calif.: Addison-Wesley.

Calvin, W. (1996). *How Brains Think.* New York: Basic Books.

Capaldi, E.J., and I. Neath. (1995). "Remembering and Forgetting as Context Discrimination." *Learning and Memory* 2, 3–4:107–132.

Carey, J. (1991). "Sleep and Dreaming." Pamphlet in a series called "Brain Concepts" published by Society for Neuroscience, Washington, D.C.

Christianson, S. (1992). "Emotional Stress and Eyewitness Memory: A Critical Review." *Psychological Bulletin* 112, 2: 284–309.

Chugani, H.T. (1991). "Imaging Human Brain Development with Positron Emission Tomography." *Journal of Nuclear Medicine* 32, 1: 23–26.

Churchland, P. (1995). *Engine of Reason: Seat of the Soul.* Boston, Mass.: MIT Press.

Clarke, D. (September 1, 1980). "Spinning Therapy Calms Hyperactivity, Accelerates Physical Development." *Brain/Mind Bulletin* 5, 20B: 2–4.

Cleeland, L. (1984). "Vestibular Disorders—Learning Problems and Dyslexia." *Hearing Instruments* 35, 8: 9F.

Colvin, R.L. (July 19, 1996). "If Students Are Paid, Test Scores Rise, Study Finds." *Los Angeles Times,* p. B-1.

Connors, K. (1989). *Feeding the Brain.* New York: Plenum Press.

Coward, A. (1990). *Pattern Thinking.* New York: Praeger Publishers.

Cytowic, R. (1993). *The Man Who Tasted Shapes.* New York: Time Warner.

Damasio, A. (1994). *Descartes' Error.* New York: Putnam and Sons.

Davidson, R.J., and S.K. Sutton. (1995). "Affective Neuroscience: The Emergence of a Discipline." *Current Opinion in Neurobiology* 5, 2: 217–224.

Davis, J. (1997). *Mapping the Mind.* Secaucus, N.J.: Carol Publishing Group.

Debes, J. (December 1974). "The Power of Visuals." *Instructor Magazine,* 84.

Deci, E., E.R. Vallerand, L.G. Pelletier, and R.M. Ryan. (Summer-Fall 1991). "Motivation and Education: The Self-Determination Perspective." *Educational Psychologist* 26, 3–4: 325–346.

DePorter, B., and M. Hernacki. (1992). *Quantum Learning.* New York: Dell Paperbacks.

Diamond, M.C. (1967). "Extensive Cortical Depth Measurements and Neuron Size Increases in the Cortex of Environmentally Enriched Rats." *Journal of Comparative Neurology* 131: 357–364.

Diamond, M., and J. Hopson. (1998). *Magic Trees of the Mind.* New York: Dutton Books, Penguin-Putnam Group.

Dowling, W.J. (1993). "Procedural and Declarative Knowledge in Music Cognition and Education." In *Psychology and Music: The Understanding of Melody and Rhythm*, edited by T.J. Tighe and W.J. Dowling. Hillsdale, N.J.: Lawrence Erlbaum and Associates.

Druckman, D., and J.A. Sweets. (1988). *Enhancing Human Performance: Issues, Theories, and Techniques*. Washington, D.C.: National Academy Press.

Dryden, G., and J. Vos. (1994). *The Learning Revolution*. Rolling Hills, Calif.: Jalmar Press.

Dudai, Y. (January/February 1997). "How Big Is Human Memory, or On Being Just Useful Enough." *Learning and Memory* 3, 5: 341–365.

Edelston, M., ed. (1995). "Did You Know That?" Column in *Bottom Line Personal* 16, 1:7.

Elias, M. (December 11, 1996). "Ritalin Use Up Among Youth." *USA Today*, p. D1.

Epstein, H. (1986). "Stages in Human Brain Development." *Developmental Brain Research* 30: 114–119.

Eysenck, M. (1994). *The Blackwell Dictionary of Cognitive Psychology*. Oxford, U.K.: Blackwell Publishers.

Fisher, R. (1990). "Why the Mind Is Not in the Head but in Society's Connectionist Network." *Diogenes* 151, 1: 1–28.

Ford, M. (1992). *Motivating Humans*. Newbury Park, Calif.: Sage Publications.

Franz, R.L. (1961). "The Origin of Form Perception." *Scientific American* 204: 66.

Freeman, W. (1995). *Societies of Brains*. Hillsdale, N.J.: Lawrence Erlbaum and Associates.

Fuchs, J.L., M. Montemayor, and W.T. Greenough. (1990). "Effect of Environmental Complexity on the Size of Superior Colliculus." *Behavioral and Neural Biology* 54, 2: 198–203.

Gardell, J. (October 7, 1997). Personal conversation.

Gardner, H. (1983). *Frames of Mind*. New York: Basic Books.

Gardner, H. (1993). *Multiple Intelligences: The Theory in Practice*. New York: Basic Books.

Gazzaniga, M. (1988). *Mind Matters: How Mind and Brain Interact to Create Our Conscious Lives*. Boston: Houghton-Mifflin/MIT Press.

Gazzaniga, M. (1997). *Conversations in the Cognitive Neurosciences*. Cambridge, Mass.: MIT Press.

George, K. (1996). "Attention Deficit: Nature, Nurture, or Nicotine?" *Journal of NIH Research* 8, 11: 24–26.

Gilbert, A.G. (1977). *Teaching the Three R's Through Movement Experiences*. New York: Macmillan Publishing.

Giles, M.M. (November 1991). "A Little Background Music Please." *Principal Magazine*, 41–44.

Gislason, S. (1996). *Getting Better with Nutritional Therapy*. Vancouver, B.C.: Enviromed Research.

Goleman, D. (1995). *Emotional Intelligence*. New York: Bantam Books.

Green, E.J., W.T. Greenough, and B.E. Schlumpf. (1983). "Effects of Complex or Isolated Environments on Cortical Dendrites of Middle-Aged Rats." *Brain Research* 264: 233–240.

Greenberg, D. (Winter 1991). "Learning Without Coercion: Sudbury Valley School." *Mothering*: 102–105.

Greenfield, S. (1995). *Journey to the Centers of the Mind*. New York: W.H. Freeman Company.

Greenfield, S. (1997). *The Human Brain: A Guided Tour*. New York: Basic Books/Harper Collins.

Greenough, W. (March 20, 1997). Personal conversation.

Greenough, W.T., and B.J. Anderson. (1991). "Cerebellar Synaptic Plasticity: Relation to Learning Versus Neural Activity." *Annals of the New York Academy of Science* 627: 231–247.

Gunnar, M., and C. Nelson, eds. (1992). *Developmental Behavioral Neuroscience* Vol. 24, pp. 155–200. Minnesota Symposia on Child Psychology. Hillsdale, N.J.: Lawrence Erlbaum Associates, Inc.

Hancock, L. (February 19, 1996). "Why Do Schools Flunk Biology?" *Newsweek*, 58–59.

Hannaford, C. (1995). *Smart Moves*. Arlington, Va.: Great Ocean Publishing Co.

Hanshumacher, J. (1980). "The Effects of Arts Education on Intellectual and Social Development: A Review of Selected Research." *Bulletin of the Council for Research in Music Education* 61, 2: 10–28.

Harth, E. (1995). *The Creative Loop*. Reading, Mass.: Addison-Wesley.

Healy, J. (1990). *Endangered Minds: Why Our Children Can't Think*. New York: Simon and Schuster.

Healy, J. (1994). *Your Child's Growing Mind*. New York: Doubleday.

Hennessy, J.W., M.G. King, T.A. McClure, and S. Levine. (1977). "Uncertainty as Defined by the Contingency Between Environmental Events and the Adrenocortical Response." *Journal of Comparative Physiology* 91: 1447–1460.

Heybach, J.P., and J. Vernikos-Danellis. (1979). "Inhibition of Adrenocorticotrophin Secretin During Deprivation-Induced Eating and Drinking in Rats." *Neuroendricrinology* 28: 329–338.

Hittman, J., ed. (Summer 1996). "Personality: It's in the Genes." *BrainWaves Newsletter*.

Hobson, J.A. (1994). *Chemistry of Conscious States*. Boston, Mass.: Little, Brown and Co.

Hooper, J., and D. Teresi. (1986). *The Three Pound Universe: The Brain, from Chemistry of the Mind to New Frontiers of the Soul*. New York: Dell Publishing.

Horn, G. (1991). "Learning, Memory, and the Brain." *Indian Journal of Physiology and Pharmacology* 35, 1: 3–9.

Houston, J. (1982). *The Possible Human: A Course in Enhancing Your Physical, Mental, and Creative Abilities.* Los Angeles, Calif.: Jeremy Tarcher.

Howard, P. (1994). *Owner's Manual for the Brain.* Austin, Tex.: Leornian Press.

Hurwitz, I., P.H. Wolff, B.D. Bortnick, and K. Kokas. (1975). "Nonmusical Effects of the Kodaly Music Curriculum in Primary Grade Children." *Journal of Learning Disabilities* 8, 2: 45–51.

Hutchinson, M. (1994). *MegaBrain Power.* New York: Hyperion Books.

Isaacs, K.R., et al. (1992). "Exercise and the Brain: Angiogenesis in the Adult Rat Cerebellum After Vigorous Physical Activity and Motor Skill Learning." *Journal of Cerebral Blood Flow and Metabolism* 12, 1: 110–119.

Jacobs, B., M. Schall, and A.B. Scheibel. (1993). "A Quantitative Dendritic Analysis of Wernicke's Area in Humans: Gender, Hemispheric, and Environmental Factors." *Journal of Comparative Neurology* 327, 1: 97–111.

Jacobs, W.J., and L. Nadel. (1985). "Stress-Induced Recovery of Fears and Phobias." *Psychological Review* 92, 4: 512–531.

Jermott, J., and K. Magloire. (1985). "Student Stress Lowers Immunity." *Journal of Personality and Social Psychology* 55: 803–810.

Jones, B.F., J. Pierce, and B. Hunter. (December 1988/ January 1989). "Teaching Students to Construct Graphic Representations." *Educational Leadership* 46, 4: 20–25.

Kagan, J.M. (1994). *Galen's Prophecy.* New York: Basic Books.

Kearney, P. (August 3, 1996). "Brain Research Shows Importance of Arts in Education." *The Star Tribune,* p. 19A.

Kempermann, G., H.G. Kuhn, and F. Gage. (April 1997). "More Hippocampal Neurons in Adult Mice Living in an Enriched Environment." *Nature* 38: 493–495.

Kinoshita, H. (1997). "Run for Your Brain's Life." *BrainWork* 7, 1: 8.

Klein, R., D. Pilon, S. Prosser, and D. Shannahoff-Khalsa. (October 23, 1986). "Nasal Airflow Asymmetries and Human Performance." *Biological Psychology* 2: 127–137.

Klein, R., and R. Armitage. (June 1979). "Rhythms in Human Performance." *Science* 204, 4399: 1326–1328.

Koch, C. (January 16, 1997). "Computation and the Single Neuron." *Nature* 385, 6613: 207–210.

Kohn, A. (1993). *Punished by Rewards.* New York: Houghton Mifflin.

Kolb, B., and I.Q. Whishaw. (1990). *Fundamentals of Human Neuropsychology.* New York: W.H. Freeman and Co.

Kosslyn, S. (1992). *Wet Mind.* New York: Simon and Schuster.

Kotulak, R. (April 13, 1993). "Research Discovers Secrets of How Brain Learns to Talk." *Chicago Tribune,* Section 1, pp. 1–4.

Kotulak, R. (1996). *Inside the Brain.* Kansas City, Mo.: Andrews and McMeel.

Kovalik, S. (1994). *ITI: The Model-Integrated Thematic Instruction.* Kent, Wash.: Books for Educators.

LaBerge, D. (1995). *Attentional Processing.* Cambridge, Mass.: Harvard University Press.

Lamb, S.J., and A.H. Gregory. (1993). "The Relationship Between Music and Reading in Beginning Readers." *Educational Psychology* 13, 2: 19–26.

Lasley, E. (1997). "How the Brain Learns and Remembers." *BrainWork* 7, 1: 9.

Lazarus, R., and B. Lazarus. (1995). *Passion and Reason.* New York: Oxford University Press.

LeDoux, J. (April 1992). "Brain Mechanisms of Emotions and Emotional Learning." *Current Opinion in Neurobiology* 2, 2: 191–197.

LeDoux, J. (December 20, 1993). "Emotional Memory Systems in the Brain." *Behavioral Brain Research* 58, 1–2: 69–79.

LeDoux, J. (1994). "Emotion, Memory, and The Brain." *Scientific American* 270, 6: 50–57.

LeDoux, J. (1996). *The Emotional Brain.* New York: Simon and Schuster.

Levine, S., and C. Coe. (1989). "Endocrine Regulation." In *Psychosomatic Medicine,* edited by S. Cheren, pp. 342–344. Madison, Conn.: International Universities Press, Inc.

MacLean, P. (1990). *The Triune Brain in Education.* New York: Plenum Press.

Maier, S., and J. Geer. (1968). "Alleviation of Learned Helplessness in a Dog." *Journal of Abnormal Psychology* 73: 256–262.

Mandelblatt, M. (December 1993). "Mostly Mozart." *Mensa Bulletin* 12: 13.

Manning, A., ed. (August 8, 1997). "Physical Skills Take 6 Hours to Sink In." *USA Today,* p. 4D.

Mark, V. (1989). *Brain Power.* Boston, Mass.: Houghton-Mifflin.

Marquis, J. (October 17, 1996). "A Real Brain Teaser." *Los Angeles Times*, p. B-2.

Martens, F. (March 1982). "Daily Physical Education—A Boon to Canadian Elementary Schools." *Journal of Physical Education, Recreation, and Dance* 53, 3: 55–58.

Matthews, R.C. (1977). "Semantic Judgments as Encoding Operations: The Effects of Attention to Particular Semantic Categories on the Usefulness of Interim Relations in Recall." *Journal of Experimental Psychology: Human Learning and Memory* 3, 8: 160–173.

McGaugh J.L., L. Cahill, and J.B. Introini-Collison. (1990). "Involvement of the Amygdaloid Complex in Neuromodulatory Influences on Memory Storage." *Neuroscience and Biobehavioral Reviews* 14, 4: 425–431.

McGaugh, J.L., L. Cahill, M.B. Parent, M.H. Mesches, K. Coleman-Mesches, and J.A. Salinas. (1995). "Involvement of the Amygdala in the Regulation of Memory Storage." In *Plasticity in the Central Nervous System: Learning and Memory,* edited by J.L. McGaugh, F. Bermudez-Ratton, and R.A. Prado-Alcala. Hillsdale, N.J.: Erlbaum and Associates.

McGraw, M. (1989). "Art Therapy with Brain-Injured Patients." *American Journal of Art Therapy* 28: 37–44.

McGregor, T. (Summer 1994). "Starting School." *BrainGym Journal* 8, 2: 4–5.

Mehler, J., and E. Dupoux. (1994). *What Infants Know.* Cambridge, Mass.: Blackwell Publishers.

Michaud, E., and R. Wild. (1991). *Boost Your Brain Power.* Emmaus, Pa.: Rodale Press.

Middleton, F., and P. Strick. (October 21, 1994). "Anatomical Evidence for Cerebellar and Basal Ganglia Involvement in Higher Brain Function." *Science* 226, 5184: 458–461.

Miller, N., and L. Melamed. (February 1989). "Neuropsychological Correlates of Academic Achievement." Poster presentation, International Neuropsychological Society, Vancouver, B.C.,

Mineka, S., M. Cook, and S. Miller. (1984). "Fear Conditioned with Escapable and Inescapable Shock: The Effects of a Feedback Stimulus." *Journal of Experimental Psychology: Animal Behavior Processes* 10: 307–323.

Mohanty, B., and A. Hejmadi. (March 1992). "Effects of Intervention Training on Some Cognitive Abilities of Preschool Children." *Psychological Studies* 37, 1: 31–37.

Morris, P.E., and N. Cook. (1978). "When Do First Letter Mnemonics Aid Recall?" *British Journal of Educational Psychology* 48: 22–28.

Murphy, M. (1992). *The Future of the Body.* Los Angeles: Jeremy Tarcher Publ.

Nadia, S. (December 15, 1993). "Kids' Brain Power." *The Oregonian, Portland.*

Nakamura, K. (1993). "A Theory of Cerebral Learning Regulated by the Reward System." *Biological Cybernetics* 68, 6: 491–498.

Oakhill, J. (1988). "Time of Day Affects Aspects of Memory." *Applied Cognitive Psychology* 2: 203–212.

Ornstein, R., and D. Sobel. (1987). *The Healing Brain and How It Keeps Us Healthy.* New York: Simon and Schuster.

Ostrander, S., and L. Schroeder. (1991). *SuperMemory.* New York: Carroll and Graf Publishers.

Overton, D.A. (1984). "State-Dependent Learning and Drug Discriminations." In *Handbook of Psychopharmacology,* Vol. 18, edited by L.L. Iverson, S.D. Iverson, and S.H. Snyder. New York: Plenum.

Palmer, L. (October 1997). Personal communication.

Palmer, L. (September 1980). "Auditory Discrimination Through Vestibulo-Cochlear Stimulation." *Academic Therapy* 16, 1: 55–70.

Parente, R., and J. Anderson-Parente. (1991). *Retraining Memory: Techniques and Applications.* Houston: CSY Publishing.

Parnell, D. (March 1996). "Cerebral Context." *Vocational Educational Journal* 71, 3: 18–21.

Pearce, J.C. (1992). *Evolutions's End.* San Francisco: Harper Collins.

Pert, C. (1997). *Molecules of Emotion.* New York: Charles Scribner's Sons.

Peterson, C., S. Maier, and M. Seligman. (1993). *Learned Helplessness.* New York: Oxford University Press.

Pollatschek, J., and F. Hagen. (1996). "Smarter, Healthier, Happier." International Health, Racquet, and Sportsclub Association Booklet, Boston, Mass.

Prescott, J. (1977). "Phylogenetic and Ontogenetic Aspects of Human Affectional Development." In *Selected Proceedings of the 1976 International Congress of Sexology*, edited by R. Gemme and C. Wheeler. New York.: Plenum.

Rauscher, F.H., G.L. Shaw, L.J. Levine, K.N. Ky, and E.L. Wright. (1993). "Music and Spatial Task Performance." *Nature* 365: 611.

"Reading at Home." (October 17, 1996). Louis Harris Poll in *USA Today*, p. 3A.

Restak, R. (1979, 1988). *The Brain.* New York: Warner Books.

Restak, R. (1994). *The Modular Brain.* New York: Charles Scribner's Sons.

Restak, R. (1993). *Receptors*. New York: Bantam Books.

Richardson, L. (January 3, 1996). "Teens Are Not Early Risers by Nature." *San Diego Union Tribune*, E-1.

Richardson, S. (1996). "Tarzan's Little Brain." *Discover Magazine* 17, 11: 100–102.

Rossi, E.L., and D. Nimmons. (1991). *The 20-Minute Break: Using the New Science of Ultradian Rhythms.* Los Angeles: Tarcher.

Rozanski, A. (1988). "Mental Stress and the Induction of Silent Ischmia in Patients with Coronary Artery Disease." *New England Journal of Medicine* 318, 4/21: 1005.

Saltus, R. (January 15, 1997). "Lost Mice Lead Way to Major Find on Memory." *The Brain in the News.* The Dana Alliance for Brain Initiatives Newsletter 4, 1.

Schab, F.R. (1990). "Odors and the Remembrance of Things Past." *Journal of Experimental Psychology, Learning, Memory, and Cognition* 16: 648–655.

Schacter, D.L. (1992). Understanding Implicit Memory. *American Psychologist* 47, 4: 559–569.

Schacter, D. (1996). *Searching for Memory: The Brain, the Mind, and the Past.* New York: Basic Books.

Scroth, M., et al. (January 1993). "Role of Delayed Feedback on Subsequent Pattern Recognition Transfer Tasks." *Contemporary Educational Psychology* 18, 1: 15–22.

Shreeve, J. (May 3, 1996). "Possibly New Skeleton Gives Path from Trees to Ground an Odd Turn." *Science* 272, 5262: 654.

Siegfried, T. (August 18, 1997). "Scientists Aren't Too Depressed About Learning from Mistakes." *Dallas Morning News,* p. 9D.

Silverman, S. (1993). "Student Characteristics, Practice, and Achievement in Physical Education." *Journal of Educational Research* 87, 1:

Simmons, S. (December 1995). "Drawing as Thinking." *Think Magazine*: 23–29

Soloveichik, S. (May 1979). "Odd Way to Teach, But It Works." *Soviet Life Magazine*: 5.

Squire, L. (1992). "Memory and the Hippocampus: A Synthesis from Findings with Rats, Monkeys, and Humans." *Psychological Review* 99, 2: 195–231.

Strasburger, V.C. (1992). "Children, Adolescents, and Television." *Pediatrics in Review* 13, 4: 144–151.

Tallal, P., S. Miller, and R.H. Fitch. (1993). "Neurobiological Basis for Speech: A Case for the Preeminence of Temporal Processing." *Annals of the New York Academy of Sciences* 682: 27–47.

Thal, D.J., and S. Tobias. (1992). "Communicative Gestures in Children with Delayed Onset of Oral Expressive Vocabulary." *Journal of Speech and Hearing Research* 35, 6: 1281–1289.

Thal, D.J., S. Tobias, and D. Morrison. (1991). "Language and Gesture in Late Talkers: A 1-Year Follow-Up." *Journal of Speech and Hearing Research* 34, 3: 604–612.

Thompson, R. (1993). *The Brain*. New York: W.H. Freeman Company.

Tonge, B.J. (1990). "The Impact of Television on Children and Clinical Practice." *Australian and New Zealand Journal of Psychiatry* 24, 4: 552–560.

Trice, A.D. (December 1982). "Ratings of Humor Following Experience with Unsolvable Tasks." *Psychological Reports* 51, 3, Pt. 2: 1148.

Turkington, C. (1996). *The Brain Encyclopedia*. New York: Facts on File.

Urich, R.S. (1984). "View Through a Window May Influence Recovery from Surgery." *Science* 224: 420–421.

Van Dyke, D.C., and A.A. Fox. (1990). "Fetal Drug Exposure and Its Possible Implications for Learning in the Pre-School and School-Age Population." *Journal of Learning Disabilities* 23, 3: 160–163.

Viadero, D. (November-December 1995). "Sleepy Heads." *Teacher Magazine*: 24–26.

"Video Games." (November 18, 1996). Survey in *USA Today*, p. 3A.

Vincent, J.D. (1990). *The Biology of Emotions*. Cambridge, Mass.: Basil Blackwell.

Wallis, D. (May 1996). "I'm Sorry, Sir—He's Out at His Desk." *Esquire*: 42.

Weinberger, N. (Fall 1994). *Music and Science Information Computer Archive Newsletter* I, 2: 3.

Weinberger, N. (Fall 1995). "Non Musical Outcomes of Music Education." *Musica Journal* II, 2: 6.

Weinberger, N. (Spring 1996). *Music and Science Information Computer Archive Newsletter* III, 1: 1.

Wickelgren, I. (December 11, 1996). "Mice Flies Point Way to Molecule That Makes Memories." *San Diego Union-Tribune,* p. E-3.

Wilder, R. (1996). "Peering into the Hyperactive Brain." *BrainWork Newsletter* 6, 5: 7.

Williams, R. (September 3, 1977). "Why Children Should Draw: The Surprising Link Between Art and Learning." *Saturday Review*: 11–16.

Wilson, D.A., J. Willner, E.M. Kurz, and L. Nadel. (1986). "Early Handling Increases Hippocampal

Long-Term Potentiation in Young Rats." *Behavioral Brain Research* 21, 223–227.

Wlodkowski, R. (1985). *Enhancing Adult Motivation to Learn*. San Francisco, Calif.: Jossey-Bass Publishers.

Woteki, C.E., and P.R. Thomas, eds. (1992). *Eat Right, Be Bright*. New York: St. Martin's Press.

Wurtman, J. (1986). *Managing Your Mind and Mood Through Food*. New York: Harper/Collins.

Wynn, K. (1990). "Children's Understanding of Counting." *Cognition* 36, 2: 155–193.

Wynn, K. (August 1992). "Addition and Subtraction by Human Infants." *Nature* 358, 6389: 749–750.

Young, L.D., and J.M. Allin. (1986). "Persistence of Learned Helplessness in Humans." *Journal of General Psychology*. 113, 1: 81–88.

Follow-Up Resources

Brain-Compatible Training Certification: Eric Jensen conducts six-day workshops and in-depth programs called "Brain-Compatible Facilitator Training." This practical staff development program develops cost-efficient, long-lasting, in-house resources. For free information and video, fax your request to (619) 642-0404. Call (888) 63-TRAIN or send e-mail to jlcbrain@connect net.com

Catalog of Brain-Compatible Resources ("The Brain Store"). Includes newest cutting-edge books, videos, audios, hands-on manipulatives, and more. Call 800-325-4769, fax 619-546-7560. Contact address: The Brain Store, 4202 Sorrento Valley Blvd., Suite B, San Diego, CA 92121.

Index

Page numbers followed by "*f*" refer to figures.

About the Author

A former teacher and current member of the International Society of Neuroscience, **Eric Jensen** has taught at all levels, from elementary through university level. He's listed in *Who's Who Worldwide*. In 1981, Jensen cofounded SuperCamp, the nation's first and largest brain-compatible learning program for teens, now with more than 20,000 graduates. He wrote *Student Success Secrets, Brain-Based Learning, Brain-Compatible Strategies, The Learning Brain,* and *SuperTeaching.* He remains deeply committed to making a positive, significant, lasting difference in the way the world learns. Jensen currently speaks at conferences and does trainings and consulting internationally. Phone (619) 642-0400. E-mail: jlcbrain@connectnet.com.

Date Due

10/30	AG 29 '05	NO 0 4 '08	
	FE 04 '06		
1/21/00	3/18/06		
	OC 25 '06		
MAR 13 2000	JA 2 '07		
OC 22 '00	AG 30 '07		
	OC 11 '07		
AG 06 '01	MR 16 '09		
SE 25 '01	APR 13 2009		
8/15/02			
SEP 02 2002			
JA 12 '03	5/31/11		
SE 05 '03			
AP 2 '04			
AP 7 '05			